Self Publishing For Canadians

Jennifer Samson

ISBN: 978-1-988797-21-2

Published by Ariesrising Media
Updated October 8, 2022

www.arieswriting.com

Cover image by Viktoriya Yakubouskaya.

Introduction

The information in this book is as up-to-date as possible and this current iteration is from October 8, 2022. Self publishing is always changing, and from month-to-month there are new players, new promotions, rule changes, added features and everything in between. This information is accurate as of the publishing date, and I'll be making an effort to keep it updated as things change. If you find any wildly outdated information, incorrect information, you have a question, or there's something you'd like me to add, please contact me at arieswriting@gmail.com or via my website at arieswriting.com.

Thank you, and I hope this book helps you sort out the often confusing world of self publishing.

1

Self publishing has existed since the dawn of the printing press. The list of successful self published authors is long and includes names like James Redfield (*The Celestine Prophecy*), Amanda Hocking (*Trylle Trilogy*), E.L. James (*Fifty Shades of Grey* series), and Andy Weir (*The Martian*).

Whether your goal is to become an Amazon bestseller, hold a printed copy of your own book, or just get your work out there for the fun of it, this book can help you navigate the confusing world of publishing and hopefully clarify a few issues you'll run across as a Canadian.

Canadians have a bit more to think about when it comes to self publishing. Most of the print-on-demand (POD) companies you will deal with will be U.S.-based, so you'll need to think about things like taxes, withholding and payment—issues American authors don't have to worry about in the same way.

The first question many people ask is "Is this going to cost me money?"

The answer? Probably.

The good news is that the amount is up to you.

While it's free to get your books on Amazon, Kobo and all major bookselling sites, you may have to pay to get your book looking professional with covers and interior formatting. How much it costs will depend on your own skill and willingness to learn or how much you are willing to spend. The other expense will be marketing. Paying for promotions and ads may be the only way you can get readers to find your book. You'll have to determine how much you're willing to spend to get your book moving up the sales charts.

One of the best ways to advertise your book is to write another— the more books you have in your backlist, the more you sell. Some authors even wait until they have three or four books in a series before publishing the first one.

But that's all in the future. For now, let's focus on the steps of self publishing a book in general so you can see what you're in for.

The Steps of Self Publishing A Book

While this list is long and daunting, so is the publishing process, so buckle up.

Write Your Book

If you've never written a book before, I highly recommend National Novel Writing Month. In the 30 days of November, you attempt to write a 50,000 word novel along with a bunch of other crazy people. Nano is a great tool because so many others are trying to write a book, many for the first time. There's lots of encouragement and fun involved, and it takes the pressure off when it's a fun group activity. Nanowrimo also hosts two other events—Camp Nano in April and July, where the rules are more lax and you can write, or edit, however much you want. Nano is really trying to be a year-round destination for writing and their new website allows you to work on, and track, projects any time of the year.

If you want to delve into a draft right now, no waiting, open up that Word, LibreOffice, Google Doc, Scrivener or even Notepad file and get to it!

A Special Note on Spelling and Language Use

One of the first decisions you'll have to make is one American authors never think about—do you use Canadian or American spelling in your book?

Neighbour or neighbor? Counsellor or counselor? Is advertise or advertize Canadian? Are readers really going to notice? Honestly, they might. Unfortunately I've seen a few non-American writers get dinged in reviews for their spelling, only to discover it was because they used Canadian or British spellings. I've also seen the opposite—readers who picked up a book set in Australia with Australian characters, but using U.S. terms and spellings, and they were upset because it wasn't authentic. We get a little more leeway since a lot of things are similar in the U.S. and Canada, but keep in mind that some readers want the experience of something different when you set your book in a particular place.

So what do you do? For me, I decide based on my book. U.S. setting with American characters? I'll use American spelling (and yes, it kills me a little inside). If the book is set in Canada, but I think I'll have a big American audience, I'll include a note that I'm Canadian and use Canadian spellings.

You may decide to use Canadian spellings no matter what, with or without a note—that's fine. Just be aware that a review talking about spelling errors may not be talking about legitimate ones. One thing I make sure to do is be consistent. If I use Canadian spellings, I make sure they are all Canadian. The site ***Canadian, British and American Spelling*** at www.lukemastin.com/testing/spelling contains a list of common words that have different spellings in Canada, the U.K. and U.S. and can help you keep everything consistent.

One other thing to be aware of—Canadianisms. Some word choices will give you away as Canadian, which is great if your book is set in Bella Coola, B.C., but not great if it's set in South Florida. I'm not talking about the obvious ones like hoser and eh, but the word choices you may not realize are different. You may need to be clear about what a mickey is, know that Americans tend to say physical therapy and not physiotherapy, that homo milk is eyebrow raising south of the border, that a parkade is a parking garage in the U.S., and an American probably won't be lacing up their runners. If you have a U.S. set book, have an American friend make sure you haven't used a Canadian term for something (like when I got dinged for using tow truck when the American city my book was set in uses the term wrecker).

So you decide and soldier on with your draft. Days, weeks or months (let's hope it's not years!) later you finish. Take a deep breath—you wrote a book!

Edit Your Book

Before handing the book over to a professional editor, I edit the book myself. At this point I'm trying to get the book to a place where I feel good showing it to my editor. This can take months for me, which is not ideal. Lots of re-writing happens with changes to plot and sometimes new scenes are added.

Some people are good at editing while they write … I am not one of these people. I'm a fast writer, but the downside is I usually have a lot to clean up after. For a free checklist of things to look over, check out the post on my blog at arieswriting.com called *Self Publishing For Canadians - The Editing List.* The password is 'ohcanada' (without the quotes).

Find an Editor

You can hire one editor or many, depending on what you want and what they offer. I always recommend new authors get a professional edit, because it will open your eyes to flaws in your writing and help you get better and better. Visit some writing message boards or Google to search for an editor or get a recommendation.

Structural, developmental or content editors will go over a manuscript for the big stuff like characters and plot. Line editors will go over the text for everything from overly flowery description to improper sentence construction and misused words. A copyeditor will check your grammar, punctuation and spelling, while a proofreader will do that final look over to make sure everything is in order. Some editors offer all of these services, some only one or two. You may decide you only want to have a line edit done, and that's fine. Just make sure you get someone with professional editing eyes to look over your book. Try not to get a friend or family member unless you know they will be 100% honest with you. There *will* be problems in your book, you *are* doing something wrong, and you need to know what those things are.

So now you've sent your baby off and you relax for a little bit. You might want to take this time to set up an author website for yourself (try wordpress.com for free options) or your author social media accounts (see chapter 2). Or if you're a real keener, you get to work on your next book.

Apply Your Edits

This is usually a good stage ... well, after you have a tiny mental breakdown when you see everything your editor flagged. You dive into fixing things and adjusting your book, and you can see it's getting better and better.

Depending on how your editor works, they may give you the document with changes in document tracking and that is that and it's up to you to decide what to do, or you may go back and forth with your editor on the changes. It all depends on the way the editor works.

But soon you get it all done and it's time to proofread. Your book should be in a near-perfect state at this point. After the final proof, you've got a clean book ready to go. But go where?

Format For Print

If you want to have a physical print book, you need to have it properly formatted so the print-on-demand company can use your file to make a book. You can hire someone to do this, but

I found it was fairly easy to do myself thanks to many Word templates for novels you can find online for free.

Most print companies want a PDF file, with fonts embedded—this means any fonts that are not standard need to be embedded into the file so the POD company can print the file with those fonts instead of standard ones like Times New Roman or Arial. This means you'll likely need to buy an interior font (a little more on that below).

I use Word, and to format I change the page size to 6x9" (there are different trim sizes, this is the one I usually use), mirror margins, include a gutter and a header/footer and set up page numbering (not fun!). After I published my first book I used that manuscript as a template and copied/pasted the new book into it to save time. That took forever, so I now write my novel drafts in a formatted document to save time. Whatever I can do to speed up the formatting process is helpful.

While you're formatting you'll have to …

Add Front Matter

Most fiction books have a title page, copyright page, and some have a dedication, all before chapter one starts. This is known as "front matter" and is all the stuff that appears before Chapter 1 starts. Get this set up. Look at books on your shelf for an idea of what information to include and how to format it.

Get an ISBN

The ISBN, or International Standard Book Number, is a number mapped to a particular format of your book. Pick up a book and check the back cover UPC code and you'll see a 10 or 13 digit ISBN (ten digit ones are common on older books). The 13 digit ones currently start with 978 or 979 and ten digit ones are no longer available. They are also usually on the inside copyright page as well.

Being Canadian, this is a cheap and easy step (more on this in Chapter 3). You need to put this number on the copyright page, so you have to get one at this stage.

Add Back Matter

Things like acknowledgements, a sample of your next book, an ad for your last book, a list of everything you've published etc.

One essential will be an author bio, because you'll need that for various print-on-demand sites that want one. So ...

Write Your Author Bio

Throw it away. Write a new one. Hate that more. Continue until you have no idea who you are anymore. Seriously, it's the worst.

Prep Your Teaser Chapter

A great marketing tool is to have a teaser chapter for your next book in the back matter. This is especially useful for series books. The downside is you may not even have a title for your sequel, forget about a first chapter.

So the best option is to write something for your next book and include that as a teaser in your current one. If it significantly changes at a later date you can always update your back matter.

So now your book is formatted! It has front matter! It has chapters and headers/footers and page numbers! It has back matter!

"Yay! The book is done!"

The book is not done.

Decide On A Typeface and Use It

Yeah, Times New Roman isn't going to cut it, sorry. It was created for newspaper and is a narrow font, so it's not suitable for books. Nothing will brand you as an amateur faster than poor Times New Roman.

There are lots of websites, like Font Squirrel, that offer free for commercial use fonts. Some great options are EB Garamond, Cardo (that's this one!), Cardiff, LibreBaskerville, Crimson, Tryst, and Theano Didot. If a font is not free for commercial use, you'll have to pay for a license. Some popular pay fonts include Adobe Caslon Pro, Bembo, ITC Baskerville, Minion Pro, Garamond, Sabon, and Dante MT. Test out a few you like, but make sure you're using serif fonts if you're writing fiction or non-fiction with a lot of text, as sans serif are harder to read in print for long stretches.

You may decide to use more than one font—a serif for the text and sans serif for titles, handwritten fonts for fun things like notes the character writes, or a font that looks like a text message from a phone. Make sure that each one you use is licensed.

Print out a few test pages to see what typeface you like best and choose one. Then choose the size you want to use. What looks best? 10 point? 11 point? Try and match size to a book on your shelf so it's not too small or too large.

Reformat the interior with the new typeface. You can use Word's Find and Replace tool (Ctrl-H) can help you change fonts en masse (use the More, then Format, then Font feature).

Now you finally get it sorted and have the interior finished.

"Yay, the – "

No.

Write the Blurb

This step is the one I stress over the most, because I suck at writing blurbs. I don't say that in a silly way. I truly suck at it. I'm the worst. I just can't summarize 80,000 – 120,000 words into a few paragraphs. My editor, on the other hand, is a genius at it. You can probably guess what I beg her to do at this point.

The blurb will go on the back cover of your print novel and in the book description everywhere you publish, so it's really important that it's exciting, describes your book and genre accurately, and makes people want to read it. Test out the blurb on others to see if they think it sounds good.

Get Covers

If you're good at Photoshop, you're lucky and you may be able to design a cover that works and looks professional. If you're like me and not talented in the Photoshop department you may need to pay for one. You'll need only a front cover for digital and both a front and back cover for print. You may also need a wraparound cover (front, spine and back) for some platforms with print.

Luckily, even though most designers charge in U.S. dollars, you can find some deals. You may be lucky and find a designer willing to do a free custom cover to build their portfolio (my book *Sin City* was designed this way). Chances are you'll have to go the pay route, and the cheapest option is usually a pre-made cover. These are covers a designer makes ahead of time and sells as-is, and all they customize is the book title and name. Pre-mades can range in price from $15 to over $200. The big range of prices guarantees you can find something in your price range. The last cover option is the most expensive—throwing some money toward a custom cover from a professional designer (perhaps custom artwork as well) and hope you make back the investment in sales.

If you're writing a series you will have to think about branding. Series covers work better when they're very similar so readers can identify them easily. A lot of pre-made cover artists will offer sets of multiple covers for a series, so you may want to look into these as an option. It might hurt to buy a lot of covers up front, but it will save you money and frustration in the long run.

Many authors buy a cover before they even write the book (or series!). They have an outline, find a great cover and try to make sure the book matches it in some way (i.e. if the cover has models, they'll make sure the character descriptions match). Other authors (hi!) choose covers after and it can be a hunt to find one that suits your book—and when you have a series it's almost impossible to match branding if you are buying covers separately. Sometimes pre-made designers will offer font changes or colour changes for an extra cost, so you can make disparate covers look more similar.

If you aren't sure if a book will become a series, make sure to take note if your pre-made designer does custom work. Some can turn a single cover into a series for extra cost. Also ask the designer about the fonts they use—you may want to use the same ones on all the books to maintain a similar look and it helps to know what they are. You can also use them in your own marketing and website (as long as you buy a license for it!).

Recommendations for covers:

Go On Write (goonwrite.com) The mock-up cover titles are really funny, so the site can be fun to search through even if you don't need a cover.

The Book Cover Designer (thebookcoverdesigner.com/product-category/premade-book-covers) Over 15,000 covers from tons of designers.

Self Pub Covers (selfpubbookcovers.com) A huge selection with affordable prices.

Convert the Print Book to PDF

Word has a built in feature to make your docx file into a PDF, but I have used doPDF converter for years. This program adds itself as a printer and allows you to embed fonts and create a PDF from any Word document.

You'll need your book in PDF form to upload it to most print platforms. Some platforms accept doc or docx, but it's nice to have a PDF you created so you can assure yourself it looks correct.

Your cover will either be a full wrap (front, back, spine) in PDF or JPG, or a separate front and back cover in JPG with the option to make a spine on the POD site for print.

Guess what? Your book is done! But only the print book. You still need to make an ePub file for digital (yes, even for Amazon). Your print book will need to be stripped of all the formatting you just did so it can be converted and look nice and clean.

Format Your Doc for ePub and Convert

You can do this yourself or pay a book formatter to do it.

I do this myself. I use Word for my books and make a copy of the book file then undo every bit of print formatting I did on the new copy. I Select All and use Clear Formatting to clear everything, then I reformat the book, making sure to change the page size back to letter (8.5x11"). I get rid of all headers and footers and page numbering since these don't matter for digital books.

For anything you want to be a chapter in your book, highlight the text and use the Heading 1 feature. Body text uses the Paragraph style. I indent slightly for each paragraph when writing fiction. It looks very boring in Word when I'm done, but ensures a clean ePub when I convert. There are many great guides online on formatting ebooks, but I recommend the Smashwords Style Guide by Mark Coker which is available for free on the Smashwords site (www.smashwords.com/books/view/52).

Be aware—if you clear formatting, it's going to clear all of your bold, italic and other text decoration as well. You'll need to make note of where to add them in again.

Once the document is formatted I use an awesome free program called Calibre to convert the docx to epub. At this stage I can edit the ePub in Calibre or another program.

Edit the ePub

Even though you converted it, there will probably be a few issues you have to fix and things you want to add. I like a program called Sigil a lot, so I use it in the final stages of my ePub prep even though Calibre has the same capabilities. I'll add clickable links in the back matter, a table of contents (required on all platforms), the cover etc, and make sure everything looks good. At this point I'll run it through ePub Validator (www.epubconversion.com/epub-validator/) to make sure it'll pass inspection when uploaded to various platforms.

Make a Mobi File?

Mobi file format was used by Kindle readers, but as of 2022, Kindle can now handle ePub files and Amazon plans to limit the ability to use mobi on its devices. That being said, some reviewers still ask for mobi at the moment, so it may be worth it to convert the file using Kindle Previewer (www.amazon.com/gp/feature.html?ie=UTF8&docId=1000765261). Just open your ePub in it and it generates a mobi for you with no work on your part whatsoever.

Upload To Your POD Companies and Choose Features

Now you have an ePub and a print book! It's time to upload them. I'm going to skip specific instructions, only because there are so many companies to choose, all with different ways of doing things.

In general, to make your ebook you'll upload the ePub and cover separately, and be asked to write a blurb, choose some keywords and categories, set the price and choose whether to release now or do a pre-order.

Print will be similar, but you'll upload a PDF or Word file of the interior and either a JPG or PDF of the covers (either separate back/front files or a wrap around). Print doesn't usually give you a pre-order option. You will have to choose things like paper colour. The choice is usually between white or cream paper.

I find white is more suitable for non-fiction books, while cream looks better for fiction (and is easier on the eyes for long reading sessions). Some platforms also allow you to choose the cover style—glossy or matte. I've tried both, and honestly can't decide which I like better, they're both really nice. I think matte tends to suit more literary works, but that's just me.

With print, you'll need to order a proof copy. When it comes, you'll find 3 spelling mistakes and 6 punctuation errors, because of course you will, even if you had the world's best editor. But now when you fix these, the changes have to be done in the print version docx (and converted to PDF again) *and* in the ePub file. Fun!

Eventually you catch no more mistakes, and you feel the book is ready to release.

Set Your Pre-order

This is an optional step. Some authors like to have a pre-order up for their digital books, allowing readers to essentially reserve a copy it before it goes on sale. On release day, they'll be sent the book automatically. Other authors prefer not to. If you don't do a pre-order, be aware that most platforms take time to make your book live. Amazon says 24 to 72 hours, while Google Play is immediate and Draft2Digital varies from taking a few hours to days to months depending on which outlets you choose to publish to through them. So if you schedule a release day and publish manually, you may want to do it a day or two in advance.

You may want to release the print book a few days or weeks in advance. Why? Because advance copy reviewers and bloggers can't leave reviews on a digital pre-order. It's nice to have reviews up ahead of time, so I post the print version live on Amazon so reviews can be left there. My print sales aren't as great as digital ones, so it doesn't spoil the launch. If you are releasing digital only, you'll have to ask your reviewers to hold their reviews until the book is live.

During the pre-order period I work on ...

Marketing

I hate marketing. Hate might be too strong a word (... it's not), as it's probably more accurate to say I'm not good at marketing. Maybe it's that old Canadian reluctance to toot my own horn, but I find trying to promote myself endlessly difficult. This is where having a marketing plan can help. I plan out all of the things I will do, from social media posts to promos, so I have a guide for the future.

Check out Chapter 5 for some information on book promotions you can look into.

I prepare a few things:

- ARC copies for bloggers/reviewers. Usually I make a notation on the copyright page that it is an ARC review copy. If it ends up on a pirating site, at least I know it was an ARC reviewer that shared it.
- Set up a mailing list (somewhere like Mailchimp or Mailerlite. See Chapter 2)
- I add a page on my website for the book (so make sure you have a website—more on that in Chapter 2).
- Send out a newsletter to my mailing list to let readers know about the release.
- Create book mock-ups for marketing. I make mock-ups with CoverVault because I can follow their Photoshop instructions, even with my limited skills.
- Social media (I already have accounts, so I start posting about the new release).
- Make sure the book and my author page on Goodreads is properly set up. (Goodreads will auto import your book from Amazon once it's released so you don't have to do this manually).
- You may want to try book trailers, Facebook ads, giveaways to build your mailing list, contests etc. Chapter 5 covers many of these.

There are as many ideas out there for marketing as there are books. Some things you can do for free, like setting up social media or targeting bloggers that accept digital books to review, but other things may cost money. Many require your book be on sale for a discount or have x amount of reviews. Now you have to chase down reviewers and save up your money.

It's trial and error for the most part. It's my least favourite part of this entire procedure, because it feels the farthest away from actually writing.

At this point, your release day arrives and your book is for sale. If you're lucky, you'll sell some books, get some reviews, and gain traction with your sales. If you're like most people, now begins the game of hustling to learn about marketing and deciding how much money to spend in order to keep your book trending upwards.

Most self published authors earn less than $500 a year. With so many books being published each year, it's very, very difficult to stand out. Chances are you'll sell some books, then see sales slow after your release. Without marketing, your book won't stay in front of the eyes of readers for long, so you may find yourself feeling more like a marketer than a writer. But hopefully, despite it all, you'll get back in front of your computer and write another book.

2

So you got an overview of what you'll be faced with if you want to self publish. Hopefully you're still here reading!

This chapter will cover a few of the basics when it comes to creating an author persona. There's only a couple things here specific to Canada.

Pen Name or Real Name?

A big choice to make when you're first setting out as an author is whether to use your real name or a pen name. A lot can go into this consideration, and there's nothing stopping you from doing both.

Some people really want to see their own, real name on the cover of a book. Maybe you have a large social media following already, or a large stable of friends and family who can buy your book and you think your own name will be easiest to leverage. Maybe you have a career in the same subject you write about so it lends authenticity. Maybe you have a great name—it could be a common one so no one can track you down, or a unique one that no one will ever confuse for anyone else. All are valid reasons to publish under your real name.

For others, a pen name is the only way to go. Maybe you're a teacher, but you write erotica and it could jeopardize your job if people knew. Maybe you don't want your friends and family to know about your books or their subject matter. Maybe you write horror under your own name, but you also have a nice middle grade book and you definitely don't want any cross over between the two. Maybe your name is hard to spell or pronounce, or it's so long it won't look good on a book cover. Maybe you share a name with an already famous author.

The downside to a pen name is if you are using one to be anonymous, you shouldn't use a free Canadian ISBN from ISBN Canada. More on that in the next chapter.

Choosing a Pen Name

If you've decided to use a pen name, great. But how do you choose one?

If you already have a pen name in mind, do a search on Amazon to see if there are other authors with the same name. If there are, consider adding an initial or changing the spelling so there's no confusion. Goodreads often assigns the wrong books to authors with the same names, so it could be a headache to keep your books separate. You might also want to check and see if the name you choose is available as a domain name or for social media accounts.

The easiest pen name is to shorten your own name. Use initials like S.E. Hinton does, or use a short form of your name if you can, like Liz instead of Elizabeth. Maybe you can use your middle name. If you're a married you can publish under your maiden name or spouse's surname or check out your mom's maiden name.

This leads right into my next suggestion—your family tree. If you need to use a pen name, but you still want to feel connected to the name you choose, this could be a great compromise. You may only need to change your surname in this case. Go back a few generations and see what surnames speak to you. This is where I get all my pen names (and a lot of character surnames, too!).

Baby name books are a great source of first names if you can't come up with any on your own, and there are some great sites out there like Nameberry to help.

Author Website

Author websites can be free or cost you an arm and a leg. You may feel they aren't necessary, but having a place where a reader can go to find out all of the information about you and your books—from an official source—is very important. You have no control over your author presence on other sites—they could shut down or require payment suddenly, change their features, require you not link to certain stores etc. On your own site you have all of the control.

There are lots of ways to get a website—free ones (like wordpress.com and blogger.com) that use free templates; pay-per-month sites like squarespace.com and wix.com have premium templates and easy site creation; or a hosted domain you usually buy per year and are responsible for setting up the entire site on your own (usually with wordpress.org).

You can make your website as simple or involved as you want. Key pages to include are your author bio, a page about your books (or a page for each book), a link to join your mailing list, a way to contact you, and, if it's your thing, a blog.

A blog allows you to share updated info about your books, your writing process, and anything else you find interesting. If your books are about a down-on-his-luck hockey player who solves murders, and you happened to play hockey, maybe you'll enjoy sharing some hockey info with your readers. If you wrote a cookbook, a food related blog would be a great draw. If you write about a fighter pilot, you can share military history. If you write about a specific location like the Yukon, Bora Bora, or Siberia, you can share interesting bits of information about your research or personal experience with it.

A blog can drive a lot of traffic to your site if you update it regularly and have something interesting to say. If you aren't into blogging, use the blog as a news page where you share the latest updates about your books and new releases, your writing progress and other interesting notes.

Domain Names

One thing you should do regardless of what type of site you choose is to buy a domain name. A domain name costs between $10–15 USD a year, and if you pick a great company you can forward the address to the free site you choose at no cost. I currently use

Google Domains to register my domain names, but I've used Dreamhost in the past as well. It's much easier to give people the address arieswriting.com than authorjennifersamson.wordpress.com.

And so we reach another decision American authors don't have to deal with. What domain extension do we get?

Do you buy authorname.com or authorname.ca? Or something else entirely, like a .net?

My preference is to always go with the .com if I can. Why? Because .com is the standard, even in Canada. People default to it and if you plan to sell outside of Canada and to attract a non-Canadian audience, people will likely forget a .ca. If someone has the .com already, you're just driving traffic to someone else's site when that happens. On the cost side, the .com is usually cheaper.

But what if the .com is taken but the .ca isn't? Honestly, I would still go with a .com—adding author, writer or books to your name. Or my choice, which was to use a screen name as my online identity. I'd only say go for the .ca if you have a Canadian centred series or you're trying to brand yourself as a Canadian writer above all. You could also buy a .ca in addition to your .com and have it forward to your main site. I also own jennifersamson.ca. It forwards you to the same site my arieswriting.com domain does— my free Wordpress site.

Early in my publishing career I had a .net. No one remembered it and it didn't look as professional, so I would definitely stay with .com and .ca.

Social Media

Social media can be a necessary evil when it comes to launching your career. Make sure you set up accounts for yourself (or your pen name). Even if you don't use them, reserving the name is a good move just so no one else can take it. So which social media should you focus on?

Facebook

A Facebook fan page is a good one to set up yourself so that you're able to control it. If a fan were to set one up one day, you wouldn't be able to edit or control any posts. Setting one up yourself allows you to be in charge of the content. While you run it from your real Facebook profile, you can post to the page as the page, hiding your real identity. You can run multiple pages, so if you have multiple pen names, you can run them all from your single Facebook account.

Facebook is also useful for its writing and publishing groups. There are many groups you can join, from genre-specific groups for writers to how-to publishing groups.

I personally gave up on having a Facebook author fan page. I have never enjoyed the publisher-side confusion, the push to advertise and the endless changes. Instead, I use my personal profile and make a post about my books public when I need to so people can follow me, but not friend me.

Twitter

Twitter is also a great platform for authors, especially for connecting with other authors. There are dozens of writing and publishing hashtags, and in addition to connecting with other writers, you can connect with readers. I am one of those authors that really prefers Twitter over Facebook, I think because Twitter is so writing-oriented. Nanowrimo is a great time to find authors on Twitter. The Nano forums have threads for sharing your Twitter handle and connecting with other writers. Most writing genres have their own hashtags and you can connect with a lot of writers and readers by reading through them and joining in. Check out the hashtags #writerscommunity #amwriting #writingtips #amediting

You can also post cover reveals, share book details and create a hashtag for your own books or series.

Goodreads

Goodreads is a book website geared toward readers. You can archive your own book library and indicate which books you've read and want to read, rate books, review them, and (my favourite)

participate in the yearly reading challenge, to challenge yourself to read X amount of books in a year.

If you sign up on Goodreads, you can convert your account to an author account, and have an author page where you can import your blog, list the books you've written, and control your author presence. You can also sign up as a Goodreads Librarian so you'll have the ability to edit information about your books. Be aware—if you want to review or rate books with an author account, everyone can see it—there's no way to make your book library hidden, so your posts and cataloguing is all public. You *can* sign up for two accounts—one to use yourself as a reader and one to use as an author. I do this, as I wanted to separate my personal reading and friends from the people I connect with as an author.

TikTok

TikTok is the newest platform authors have jumped on. "Booktok" has exploded recently. Share your book with others through short videos, or gain more of an audience by sharing favourite books, writing tips, info about your series etc. Use the hashtags #booktok, #authortok, #books, #reading, #booknerd and more.

Instagram

If you're a visually-oriented person, you may love Instagram, which is a photo posting app owned by Facebook. You can use hashtags in your photo descriptions, allowing others to discover them. You can post book covers, inspiration for your novels, and if you live in or visit real locations you write about, you can include photos.

Lots of writers love sharing snapshots of their own libraries and book collections, so you may be inspired by Instagram and be able to connect with readers and other writers there. Check out the hashtags #instabooks #writersofinstagram #shelfie #amreading #booksofinstagram

Pinterest

Pinterest is a virtual pin board where you can create a board about any subject and pin up photos and ideas related to that subject. I don't find Pinterest particularly useful for connecting with readers or other writers, but I do find it great for inspiration and story planning.

You can make your boards public or private (secret) on Pinterest. I often start secret boards for a book I'm working on and pin pictures of locations, models for my characters and other things that inspire the book and my writing. I'll make these boards public once I publish the book. I don't know if readers are interested, but I find them fun and helpful for myself.

Other Social Media

You may be really into other social media as a user, and decide they'd be great for your author social media. Some authors find success using YouTube to produce videos about writing and their books. Others want to have a professional profile on LinkedIn, or they like microblogging on Tumblr. Reddit is a great tool for connecting with other writers and for sharing your promos. Some people love Snapchat, blogging on Medium or writing freebie stories on Wattpad.

Any social media you use is up to you. You may want to remain more mysterious and not use social media at all—but do make sure you have a website for people to go to for info on your books, if nothing else.

The Mailing List

Talk to any successful self published author and almost every author will tell you that a key to success is their mailing list.

Mailing lists are pretty old school. When I first got online in the olden days of 1995, mailing lists were the primary way people communicated in groups. So it's a little strange that they are still so popular for sharing writing information, but maybe that shouldn't be the case—they are text-based, after all.

You can sign up for a free account at Mailchimp or Mailerlite to check it out. You won't be charged until you hit 2000 (Mailchimp) or 1000 (Mailerlite) subscribers (note that Mailchimp includes people who have opted out of your emails as subscribers until you physically delete them), and that can take you awhile to achieve. One thing to note about these services—they require a mailing address listed which goes out on each mailing, so again, you may want a P.O. Box so your home address isn't listed.

To get a sense of how other authors use mailing lists, check out who is top selling in your genre and join their mailing lists to see how they communicate with their readers. This goes for their social media as well. Some genres expect more interaction from authors than others, so it can be helpful to see what others are doing.

Now for the big question—how do you get people to sign up? Chapter 5 has some information on that, as well as other promotions can you do to help readers find your book.

3

Now to the nitty gritty. As an author you'll have to deal with U.S. taxes (not in the way you think), Canadian taxes (in exactly the way you think) and other considerations like ISBNs.

U.S. Withholding Taxes

When you self publish, the print-on-demand (POD) printers based in the States—like Amazon, Draft2Digital, Lulu, Smashwords etc—automatically withhold 30% of your royalty earnings for U.S. taxes. I know, you're thinking "wait, I have to pay U.S. taxes?!" No, you don't.

Canadians are very lucky—we have a tax treaty with the U.S.. The U.S./Canada Tax Treaty states in Article XII that Canadians should have 0% of their U.S. royalty earnings withheld.

This does not automatically reduce your withholding—you need to *tell* the platform not to take your money. To do this, you either complete their online tax interview (Amazon, Draft2Digital, Google Play and others do this), or you have to fill out an IRS tax form called a W8–BEN and send it to the platform (either electronically or by snail mail). Once this is on file, they will not tax your royalties in the U.S.—you do, however, have to claim them on your Canadian income tax as royalties.

The W8–BEN used to require you have an Individual Tax Identification Number (ITIN), which was a number you had to get from the IRS and involved a lot of hoop jumping (and in my case, hoofing it over the border to an IRS office), but you are now allowed to enter your Canadian SIN in its place where it says "Foreign Tax identifying numbers." Thankfully the ITIN is a thing of the past, because there is nothing more soul draining than sitting in an IRS office for hours.

Kobo is the one platform where you won't have to worry about this—they're based in Canada and don't withhold.

Canadian Taxes

You have to claim your royalties on your Canadian taxes as either royalties (Line 104 for works with no expenses associated with them) or self employed income (Line 135 for royalty works that do have expenses associated). Which you choose depends on if you're going actually going to take deductions for expenses—self employed allows you to do that, royalties does not. You'll have to determine if taking the deductions are worth it for you. (Note: I'm not a tax expert at all—I don't even like math—but this is what CRA told me. Verify yourself as I am not responsible for CRA coming for you!). Ideally, deal with a tax professional who has experience with publishing.

The best thing you can do is keep track of your income. The U.S. platforms you use should send you a 1042–S form at tax time—it's the "Foreign Person's U.S. Source Income Subject to Withholding" form. It will show how much you made in U.S. sales in U.S. dollars and how much money was withheld. The problem? Sometimes I don't receive one. It's shown in U.S. dollars. It doesn't show sales from other locations. In other words, it's a terrible way to keep track of your income.

Because of this, I keep track of my income myself, so I can report it in Canadian dollars. Everything I receive as royalties to my bank account or PayPal (the two ways I get paid) I keep track of in an Excel file so it's easy to report it at tax time. This is especially useful because other platforms, like Kobo, don't send you any paperwork. And they're Canadian!

The nice thing is almost every platform will pay directly to your back account via Electronic Funds Transfer or to PayPal where you can move it to your account, so it's easy for you to look back and see what you actually received in Canadian funds and report this.

GST Number

If you make over $30,000 a year in *Canadian* sales with your writing (congratulations, you rock star), you'll have to get a GST number. Once you have this number you'll be required to collect and pay GST to the government where applicable. Amazon.ca charges GST on physical books, but not on ebooks, and this is where you could be hit (along with sales from your own website, in person at events, etc).

My recommendation (since I'm the World's Worst At Taxes) is if you are close to making 30K in Canadian sales, get an accountant who is well versed in publishing to deal with your taxes. Keep everything, take screenshots of bank deposits etc, and make sure you hold back some of your cash in case you owe the CRA.

The ISBN

The International Standard Book Number is the 13 digit number by the bar code on each book that currently starts with 978 or 979. This is how people find your book and is mapped directly to that format of your book. If you are selling print you need this number.

You can also use an ISBN for ebooks (although Amazon and other platforms will assign their own file number to it in lieu of an ISBN – for instance, Amazon uses the ASIN – Amazon Standard Identification Number). Some print-on-demand platforms offer free ISBNs, and their ISBNs list them as the publisher of record. If you get your own ISBN, you are the publisher of record, which looks a bit more professional.

Unlike our neighbours to the south, who have to pay through the nose for ISBNs ($250 USD for ten ISBNs!), Canadian publishers get them for *free*. Score one of the maple leaf. *Finally.*

All you have to do is register with ISBN Canada (www.bac-lac.gc.ca/eng/services/isbn-canada/Pages/isbn-canada.aspx). To qualify you have to reside in Canada. If you are Canadian living overseas, you do *not* qualify.

If you are an author who publishes only in French, you can contact the Bibliothèque et Archives nationales du Québec (BAnQ) to request an ISBN that starts with 2 to indicate French language books.

When you register for your publisher account, you'll have to give the name of your publishing company. Time to have a little fun and think of a company name. This doesn't have to be a registered business yet, just a name that you'll include in your front matter as publisher. For instance, my young adult books are published by Ariesrising Media.

You'll also have to include your real name and address, as well as a phone number as a contact. If you have privacy concerns, you should consider getting a P.O. Box or registering as a business officially.

You can request a block of ISBNs at once—I started out requesting 10 at a time, but quickly ran out (you'll need one ISBN for paperback, one for ebook, another for hard cover ... it adds up). Now I request 100 at a time and they last for much longer and the numbers are all very similar.

Be aware—if you publish under a pen name and don't want anyone to know who you are, you <u>will be identifiable</u> via your Canadian ISBNs, as you are required to list a real name and address as a publisher when applying for your ISBNs. The ISBN database is <u>searchable</u>, so any books you give a Canadian ISBN to will be searchable to your registered name and address.

If you want to be truly anonymous, the best way to do that is to use the ISBN offered for free by some platforms, or use the platform assigned number (e.g. ASIN) for digital work. You wouldn't have a Canadian ISBN, but you will also be totally anonymous.

Copyrighting Your Work

Your work is automatically protected by copyright when you create it. In Canada, copyright exists for your lifetime plus 50 years following your death, after which your work enters the public domain and anyone can use it.

So why register a copyright if it's already protected?

If someone was to plagiarize your work, the certificate issued by the Canadian Intellectual Property Office can be used in court as evidence of your ownership. Without the certificate, it may be more difficult for you to prove ownership. You can copyright your book for $50 CAD online at the CIPO website.

The copyright database is searchable; however, if you wish to remain anonymous you can fill out the information with a pen name as long as you are the owner of the work as well as the author of the work. Note that the form and search require a mailing address which will be visible in the search results, so a P.O. Box specific to that pen name is probably the safest way of assuring anonymity.

Cataloguing in Publication

Cataloguing in Publication (CIP) is a free program offered to publishers that standardizes bibliographic information for books. The data appears in the Library and Archives Canada online catalogue. If you've ever noticed a block of info on the copyright page listing what categories the book falls under, you've seen CIP Data.

Unfortunately, this program is not offered to self publishers unless you send your work in to the Legal Deposit Program managed by the Library and Archives Canada. Two copies have to be sent in for each creation that has its own ISBN (and at your own cost!), and they'll create a CIP Data block for the book once that is done. The Library and Archives has information for self publishers at www.bac-lac.gc.ca/eng/services/Pages/are-you-a-self-publisher.aspx

Getting Paid

Most platforms pay out via electronic funds transfer (EFT) or use a service like PayPal.

PayPal is easy—all you need is an email address. You can add your bank account to PayPal and then transfer over your earnings. If you are paid in USD, it will enter your account in Canadian dollars (unless you have a U.S. dollar account).

EFT is free and easy, but setting up your bank account information can be a little tricky because platforms ask for certain information. You need the account type (savings, chequing), the 7-digit account number, the 3-character bank code, the 5-character branch code (also called a transit number or routing number), and name of the institution. If your account number is only 6 digits, add a zero to either the beginning or end (you'll have to test which works).

The bank codes for Canadian banks are easy to find with Google – the major banks are Bank of Montreal (001), Scotiabank (002), RBC (003), TD (004), National Bank of Canada (006), CIBC (010), and HSBC (016).

Your branch code (aka transit number, aka routing number) is 5 digits. The first four is your branch identifier and the last number depends on your location. If you only see a 4 digit branch code, visit en.wikipedia.org/wiki/Routing_number_(Canada) to get the last digit.

If you have trouble adding your account, take a screenshot to the bank and ask them what information you need.

4

Where To Publish

As a general rule there are a handful of sites you should be on if you decide not to be exclusive to Amazon digitally. The list is fairly short—Amazon, Kobo, Apple Books, Barnes and Noble and Google Play. These five (the Self Publishing Big Five, if you will) cover just about every ereader and tablet out there.

The question is, how do you get your book on these stores?

You can choose to upload directly to each site and manage your book across each site separately, or use an aggregator to get on some or all. Going direct or with an aggregator depends on many things—like how many sites you want to go between, what the aggregator or direct site offers as incentive, which sites the aggregator gets you on, the royalty amounts you'll make, and the ease of using the site.

For example, I chose to go direct with Amazon so I can access their Amazon Advertising ads and can go into the KDP Select program with some books. I also went direct with Google Play because the aggregator I chose for the rest doesn't publish to Google Play. I use Draft2Digital for the rest right now. It's up to you how you choose to publish.

You may find reference to some defunct publishing platforms online. Createspace was an Amazon company that handled print. It shut down in August 2018, and all of Amazon's print work was moved to KDP Print. Pronoun, which was run by Big Five publisher MacMillan, was another platform that closed in early 2018. Authors moved to various platforms.

Royalty splitting is not common, so if you have a co-author, Lulu and Draft2Digital are your best bets (and D2D can get you on Amazon KDP if revenue splitting is more important than the other features Amazon KDP offers). There is also a service called Abacus by Publish Drive that can split royalties from other platforms, but there is a cost associated with it.

What options are out there? Read on for an overview of the most common ones.

Amazon's Kindle Direct Publishing (KDP)

Amazon is the biggest bookstore in the world, and the Kindle reader the most popular, especially among U.S. and U.K. readers. While the Kindle is not as popular in Canada, your biggest audience may be here since people can read on their phones. Amazon is a U.S. company.

Paperback – Yes

Hardcover – Yes, case laminate

Ebook – Yes

Distributes To – Digital to Amazon.com and other countries (Canada, U.K., Australia, France, Germany, Spain, Japan, Brazil and more). Their extended print distribution gets you onto Amazon Canada, U.K., France, Japan, Germany, Spain and Italy as well as other booksellers and libraries.

Payment Splitting – No

Tax Interview

Online tax interview.

Payment Structure and Payments

Payments are made in the currency in which they were sold. U.S. payments come to you in U.S. funds, U.K. payments in British pounds etc. So this means in one month you could get multiple payments from Amazon as each currency is paid out separately.

Print is also paid separate from ebook sales.

Digital books priced under $2.99 only qualify for 35% royalties, while books above $2.99 get 70% royalties. Paperback royalties are 60% of list price, but only 40% for extended sales.

Pricing

Prices are set in U.S. dollars for the .com, but you can manage territorial prices for the other stores, including Amazon.ca. Books priced 99 cents or lower earn 35% royalties, while books over 99 cents to 9.99 earn 70% in royalties.

In December 2019 Amazon got a printer in Canada, so our books are now eligible for Prime shipping, and paperback sales show as Canadian sales (previously they showed as U.S. paperback sale). We also get a larger royalty now. Print sales show when they ship, not when they are ordered.

The Extended Distribution print gets your book in the Ingram catalogue, and allows stores outside of Amazon to order it. A sale through this avenue gives you less in royalties, as the royalty cut is also being shared with another bookseller. You also see it show up as Extended Distribution Units Shipped in your dashboard. These sales are only posted once a month, and only if you have any Extended Distribution print sales.

Pay out is via electronic funds transfer directly to your bank account. They pay out any amount, so if you earn it, you'll receive that payment, but 60 days after the sale.

Pre-orders

You can set pre-orders for ebook only, but if you miss the deadline for uploading the proper content, they will prevent you from doing pre-orders in the future. You get lots of reminder emails though.

Accepted Files

Formatted ePub, Word files, PDF files, JPG for covers

Other

- Kindle is the most popular ereader in the U.S. and Amazon the biggest bookstore, so you'll have the greatest visibility here. The Kindle reader isn't as popular in Canada, but since you can read books on the Kindle app on phones and tablets, it's been the biggest portion of my sales.

- For print you can order proof copies (that say PROOF) across them, and author copies (which you can sell at events). Author and proof copies are now available for purchase through amazon.ca since we have a Canadian printer now.

- Print sales show up on your dashboard when they ship, not when they're bought.

- Print sales of your book on the Canadian site (.ca) now show up as Canadian sales in Canadian dollars since Amazon has a Canadian printer.

- You can use their ISBNs. They offer the Amazon-based ASIN for digital books and free ISBNs for print books, so if you want to remain anonymous, that's the best way to do it.

- Digital books can be opted in to KDP Select, a program which allows your book to be part of Kindle Unlimited where subscribers can borrow the books to read as part of their membership. A share of the KDP Select Global Fund is earned based on how many pages of your book are read by readers who borrow it. Marketing perks allow you 5 days of offering your book free or 7 days of offering it on discount per Kindle Select period (which is 3 months—you can opt in and out of the program). Your book must be exclusive to Amazon to enroll and not sold elsewhere digitally.

    a. To access the deals and KU, you have to be exclusive to Kindle. This could be a deal breaker if you sell well on another platform or want your book available to Kobo readers in Canada.

b. There's been a lot of issues with KU in the last few years, from missing page reads, to bots targeting books with inflated page reads and authors gaming the system with book stuffing. You may want to test the waters to see if KU works for you, and then go wide. Or vice versa.

c. Gaining visibility in KU is just as difficult as being wide. You will still need to focus on marketing, as being in the program doesn't automatically offer any sales boost. KU success is often based on genre—some are more popular in KU than others.

- Print allows you to choose between glossy and matte covers and between white and cream interior paper. The white paper is very nice, but it tends to look more like a non-fiction book, while the cream looks better for fiction. Be aware that you are stuck with your interior paper colour choice—you can't change it after. You *can* change your cover choice, though. Amazon offers glossy or matte covers. I think both look great, so it's really personal choice in the end. If you do want to change your interior paper, you'll have to retire that book (unpublish it), get a new ISBN and upload an entirely new book and choose new options. If you've already published digitally, Amazon's help people have told me they can associate the new print book with the digital one on both your dashboard and your Amazon book page for consistency (and to separate out the retired versions so you don't accidentally update those).

- There is no way to split payments between co-authors. Kindle desperately needs to add this feature.

- You can access Amazon Advertising and run ads on your books.

- Their help system is hit or miss. They have many features which require you to contact help (price matching, linking books, adding categories) that should be automated and available for authors to control. That alone would eliminate a good portion of help requests. Your first contact email will result in a canned response from someone with no technical information and it often sounds like they never read your email. They'll pass it on and if you're lucky they'll resolve your issue. If not, you'll probably be passed between multiple people, as they don't seem to keep cases with one help person. I have had great experiences with help on platforms like Kobo and Draft2Digital, but Amazon (probably because of its sheer size) has been the most difficult to deal with, just because of the lack of consistency.

- Kindle Vella is a new program for U.S. authors (at the moment) that allows serialized stories. It's available to American customers via Kindle.

Apple Books

Apple Books (formerly Apple iBooks) is the digital bookstore for all Apple products. iPhone and iPad users can download their books here. Going direct to Apple is only possible if you are a Mac user as they use Mac-proprietary programs for upload.

Paperback – No

Hardcover – No

Ebook – Yes

Distributes To – Apple Books

Payment Splitting - No

Tax Interview

iTunes Connect has an online tax interview.

Payment Structure and Payments

Apple takes a 30% fee so you get a 70% royalty.

They allow you to add your bank account information for payments.

Pricing

Apple sells in 51 territories, but uses USD as the standard, although you can change prices based on territory in the local currency. So you can set the Canadian price in CAD and the U.K. price in pounds etc.

Pre-orders

Yes, you can set pre-orders.

Accepted Files

ePub or iBooksAuthor files submitted through iTunes Producer, which is a Mac only program.

Other Information

- iTunes Producer is the only way to submit files to Apple, and it is restricted to Apple users, so Mac only. Windows users must use an aggregator or find a way to borrow a Mac with iTunes Producer installed in order to upload their book.

- They have their own book file authoring program called iBook Author. Since I'm a Windows gal, I haven't had the experience of using this, but if you don't have an ePub prepared, this is a good option for getting on Apple.

- You get a greater royalty going direct here than through an aggregator, but it won't be a choice if you use Windows.

- They offer promo codes (250 codes for each book) that you can use to give out to reviewers and bloggers so they can get a free ARC copy of your book.

- No revenue splitting (splitting royalties between co-authors). This is pretty standard—there is only one platform that has this capability (Lulu).

- You can earn a commission on sales through their store affiliate program. These affiliate links can be used on your site so anyone who clicks and buys will earn you an extra commission on top of your royalty.

- I use an aggregator to get on Apple, but I find I get a decent amount of sales here, so it's worth it to be on this platform.

Draft2Digital (D2D)

Draft2Digital (D2D) is a U.S.-based company out of Oklahoma. They are one of platforms I currently use, and I'm very happy with them since I switched to them in 2017. They publish ebook and print and have recently acquired Smashwords and will be integrating that site into their own soon.

Paperback – In beta for some users at the moment.

Hardcover – Not currently.

Ebook – Yes

Distributes To – Amazon, Apple Books, Barnes & Noble, Kobo (including Kobo Plus), Tolino, OverDrive, Bibliotheca, Scribd, 24Symbols, Playster, Baker & Taylor and Hoopla. They used to get you on Google Play, but the Google Play pricing structure (see their entry later in the book) made it too difficult to sustain.

You can opt out of any at any time, and you can distribute to only the ones you want.

Payment Splitting – Yes. You can add one or more collaborators and divide payments at any percentage.

Tax Interview

D2D provides an online tax interview.

Payment Structure and Payments

D2D takes 15% of your net royalties. They pay out via cheque ($100 minimum), direct deposit ($10 minimum for international sent via Western Union Global Pay), PayPal ($0.01 mnimum) and Payoneer ($20 minimum).

Some digital stores pay out to D2D 60 days after the sale, but when D2D is paid by the platform they pay you that month.

Pricing

Main book pricing is in U.S. dollars, but you can set pricing for specific countries in their currency. For instance, you can make the U.S. price $4.99 and then change the Canadian price to $4.99 CAD and the Australian price to $3.99 AUD. I always like to match the Canadian price to the U.S. price, but in Canadian dollars, because I've always hated how much more books are in Canada with the exchange, so I appreciate platforms that let me do this. I also like to give breaks to other Commonwealth nations.

You can also set books priced to free, except on Amazon.

Pre-orders

Yes, you can set pre-orders everywhere except Amazon.

Accepted Files

D2D accepts Word files and formatted ePubs. If you submit a Word file they can add front and back matter for you (which you enter in separately and can change any time), and they can provide a print ready PDF for print.

Other Information

- Lots of great auto services like new release announcements, adding books to a series, publisher profiles, etc. They also have an auto back matter and front matter feature.

- When there's an issue with your book during the process, it actually tells you exactly what the problem is. This makes fixing it much easier.

- Their help department replies in a decent amount of time and handles any issues quickly.

- They assign you a free ISBN if you don't have your own, so that's great for anonymity.

- If you want to use Amazon Advertising ads or KDP Select, you can't do that through their Amazon feature, you have to be direct with Amazon for that.

- Payment splitting is a new feature as of November 2020. You can add collaborators to your books and pay out in any percentage.

- You can't see your pre-orders. Only Apple (who provides the info daily), Kobo, and Barnes and Noble (weekly estimates) provide pre-order info, and currently it's not available on your dashboard. You can contact D2D directly and they can look it up and tell you. Hopefully they can add this soon.

- Delisting a book can take awhile for Tolino subsidiaries (bol.de and Thalia) and especially with Overdrive and Bibliotheca which can take 7–10 business days. If you are pulling your books to go wide, give yourself some time to make sure they're gone.

- Hoopla can take forever to add your books. Mine took a year. I shudder to think how long it could take to remove!

- They offer URL links for books with books2read, which is a handy service that directs readers to a page for your book with links to all stores its available in— and those store links will take them to the correct country store (ie Amazon.ca over .com if it knows you're in Canada).

- They have been making a big effort to add new services and features each year.

- Their Kobo submission allows you to be in Kobo Plus and not be obligated to the 90 day commitment.

- You can't access any of the Kobo platforms special promotions or events unless you're direct to Kobo. The same goes for Amazon's KDP program and Amazon Advertising ads.

- With their acquisition of Smashwords means new sales channels will open to authors and you'll be able to sell in the Smashwords store.

Google Play

If you have a Google account, it's very easy to sign up for this publishing platform that will provide content to Android users as well as anyone who can sideload ePub. They can also be accessed via a few aggregators.

Paperback – No

Hardcover – No

Ebook – Yes

Distributes To – Google Play Store, Google Books

Payment Splitting - No

Tax Interview

Their online tax interview is very confusing. First question is "Are you a U.S. citizen?", you check no. Then it asks if you're a Corporation, Intermediary or Tax–Exempt Entity. You might assume Tax–Exempt Entity because you're an individual who doesn't have to pay withholding, but that is wrong. Choose Corporation and then indicate the income is NOT connected with your business operations in the U.S. (yes ... even though you sell books there). This gets you to the W8–BEN form you need to fill out.

Payment Structure and Payments

Google Play lets you add a Canadian bank account. They pay out once a month via EFT with a one dollar threshold.

Pricing

GooglePlay has a strange pricing structure.

They discount your book immediately, so if you want to sell for $4.99, you'll have to mark the price as $6.48 on Google Play. It'll be discounted to $4.99 immediately on the platform. Annoying, right?

Here is a chart for the conversions:

Price You Want – Price You Set

0.99 – 0.99
1.99 – 2.40
2.99 – 3.93
3.99 – 4.99
4.99 – 6.48
5.99 – 7.78
6.99 – 8.32

This chart is usually pretty accurate, but you may need to keep an eye on the discounting price to make sure it's accurate (so other platforms won't price match to it). Price changes go live immediately—there's no waiting for approval like Amazon.

You can schedule price promotions as well and indicate how long you want them to run.

Pre-orders

Yes

Accepted Files

Formatted ePub and PDF files

Other

- There's a huge Android audience out there, and this is the place many will be buying their books, so it's a good idea to get on here. There are lots of international readers as well.

- Their sales reports are only downloadable—you can't see sales on the page which I find so, so annoying. Their Excel downloads do have a lot of great information though, I just wish they would summarize your sales so you didn't have to download an Excel file just to see the numbers. Some of the downloads screw up the date. The date may show as 2019-03-30 and the next sale shows as 30-19-03, so you spend a lot of time cleaning up their Excel files. This only started happening recently.

- If you are waiting or don't have time to wait, there's only a few aggregators that can get you on Google Play at the moment—Streetlib and PublishDrive.

- You are required to make about 20% (that's the minimum) of your book available on Google Books. On the plus side it makes your book a little bit searchable and maybe more discoverable, but the downside is 20% of your book is online.

- There is no revenue splitting between co-authors.

- Google Play updates are instantaneous. From content to price changes, the minute you press submit, they go live. This is especially great for price changes.

IngramSpark

IngramSpark is a bit of a pricier option for self publishing, but there are some advantages. One of the biggest differences is that IngramSpark charges set up fees for your book, but they often have special deals that waive fees.

Paperback – Yes

Hardcover – Yes

Ebook – Yes

Distributes To – The Ingram network distributes print to Amazon, Barnes and Noble, Chapters/Indigo, Adlibris, Agapea, Aphrohead, Bertrams, Blackwell, Book Depository Ltd, Books Express, Coutts Information Services, Designarta Books, Eden Interactive, Foyles, Gardners, Trust Media Distribution, Mallory International, Paperback Shop, Superbookdeals, The Book Community, Waterstones, Wrap Distribution, Booktopia, Fishpond, The Nile, James Bennett, ALS and Peter Pal. There is also the ability for libraries, other retailers and schools to potentially order it. Ebook accesses Amazon, Kobo, Barnes and Noble, and Apple.

Payment Splitting - No

Tax Interview

Online tax information. They also have Canadian-specific tax interviews if you have a GST number.

Payment Structure and Payments

Payments made in U.S. dollars can be sent by EFT or by PayPal. If you wish to be paid in Canadian dollars, you are limited to EFT.

Pricing

Global pricing allows you to set the price in the currency of various countries, including Canada.

Pre-orders

Yes, you can set pre-orders, for both print and ebook.

Accepted Files

ePub, PDF (for print interior and cover), JPG for ebook covers

Other

- IngramSpark charges a fee to create your book. The set up fee for ebook only starts at $25/title, while print starts at $49/title.

- You can print and ship books to yourself or directly to your customers. This is handy if you sell a lot in person at conferences or want to set up a store on your site.

- You have lots of trim size choices, binding types and paper options, more than at other POD companies.

- Revisions also cost money. If you need to make a revision, it's $25 per print book or uploaded file.

- Book production costs are fairly standard in cost. Global and U.S. order covers are charged at $1.14 USD while interior pages are $0.0126 per page. For a 200 page book, it would be $3.66. Shipping fees are calculated at purchase.

- They provide a downloadable user guide for their site to help you get the most out of it. The site also offers lots of bonuses like book formatting guides, distribution and other guides.

- If you enable the ability to return books, you have a better chance of getting into stores, but if a store orders copies of your book and returns them, you're on the hook for the cost. This really hits Canadians hard, as they charge international addresses $25 per book for shipping and handling in addition to the current wholesale cost of your book, so it could be very expensive if they don't sell.

- There are often coupon deals to waive set up fees or waive fees for updating your book.

- You have to bring your own ISBN, as they don't offer any. So there's no way to be truly anonymous here.

Kobo Writing Life (KWL)

The only Canadian-based self publishing company. Rakuten Kobo sells the Kobo ereader (I love my Aura H2O!) and has a partnership with Indigo Books and Music. Chances are your Canadian friends and family are using a Kobo if they have an ereader.

Paperback – No

Hardcover – No

Ebook – Yes

Distributes To – Angus and Robertson (Australia), Collins (Australia), Livraria Cultura (Brazil), Chapters Indigo (Canada), FNAC (France, Portugal, Spain), Rakuten (France, Japan, USA), La Feltrinelli (Italy), Mondadori (Italy), Gandhi (Mexico), Libreria Porrua (Mexico), Bol (Netherlands, Belgium), PaperPlus (New Zealand), National Book Store (Philippines), La Central (Spain), D&R (Turkey), Idefix (Turkey), WHSmith (UK), American Booksellers Association (USA), Walmart (USA) and of course the Kobo.com store in many countries.

Payment Splitting - No

Tax Interview

No tax interview for Canadians as Kobo is Canadian and there is no withholding to worry about.

Note: They don't send you tax forms at tax time either.

Payment Structure and Payments

You can add your bank account information easily. Payouts are at a minimum of $50 paid via EFT 45 days after the end of each monthly period. They no longer pay out every 6 months regardless of earnings, so it could take a really long time to get your money if you use Kobo directly.

Pricing

A 70% royalty for books $2.99 and over and for under it's 45%. You can customize prices for various countries in their currency (Countries include the U.S., U.K., Australia, New Zealand, Japan and more).

You can list a book as free. You can also set sale prices to run for certain periods.

Kobo also has a promotions section where you can either pay for promotions or they'll take a cut of your sales during the promo. I had good luck with a few of these.

Pre-orders

Yes, you can set pre-orders.

Accepted Files

Doc/docx, ePub, mobi and odt.

Other

- Kobo is not as well known in the U.S., but thanks to its partnership with Indigo bookstores, had 46% of the Canadian ereader market back in 2012 (Amazon was 24% and Sony 18%. I suspect Kobo use is higher than that now since Sony quit the ereader game in 2014).

- Their Kobo readers allow downloads from the Kobo store, but you can also sideload epubs and PDFs downloaded elsewhere on the devices which means people can download books from other sources and load them on the Kobo, so they aren't restricted to the Kobo store.

- You can publish without an ISBN but some stores (Chapters, WHSmith) won't accept it. Kobo does NOT supply any ISBNs, so if you want to be anonymous you'll have to publish without one, or use an aggregator (Lulu, Smashwords, Draft2Digital) to get on Kobo, otherwise you can use get your own free ISBNs in Canada.

- Kobo ereaders use Overdrive/Libby allowing readers to take out books from their local libraries.

- You can publish to Kobo via an aggregator like Lulu or D2D, but the earnings are higher using the Kobo Writer's Life platform, which is easy to use and has a few features not found on other platforms.

- They have a program called Kobo Plus that you can opt–in to, and you do not have to be exclusive to Kobo to participate, which is great. The program is currently in Canada, Australia, New Zealand, France, Italy, the Netherlands, Belgium and Portugal and will expand to other territories. The commitment is "no fewer than 90 days". You can submit a request to have them removed prior to the 90 days.

- If your material is interesting to an American audience, you may not have a lot of sales to U.S. readers here. My sales were primarily Canada, Australia and New Zealand.

- Their help people are very helpful. I've never had an issue go on unsolved for long. They are great with communication when you have an issue.

- The sales reports need work. There are too many clicks to get where you want, and it's complicated to see all of your info. They don't have a way to export your sales info to Excel or other applications.

- No revenue splitting between co-authors, which sucks, but is the norm unfortunately

- Kobo occasionally has great programs come up—in the summer of 2019 they had a $40 deal to get your book on Netgalley to get reviews. Netgalley usually costs a small fortune, so this is a great deal.

Lulu.com

Lulu.com, a North Carolina based company, is one of the oldest self publishing platforms out there. It was the first one I used and was print only back in 2006. They offer print books, ebooks, photo books, comic books and magazines.

Paperback – Yes

Hardcover – Yes

Ebook – Yes

Distributes To – Lulu.com store, Amazon, Apple, Barnes and Noble, Kobo any retailer in the Ingram distribution network.

Payment Splitting - Yes

Tax Interview

Canadians can snail mail or FAX a W8-BEN form.

Payment Structure and Payments

Payout via PayPal by the 5th of the month. Threshold for PayPal is $5 so they'll payout after you hit that in sales.

Pricing

Prices can be listed in various currencies (USD, CAD), but it bases all other locations on this. So if you choose to list the price in USD, it converts it from USD for every other country, which sucks.

They offer some promos—you can discount your book yourself (it'll hit you in the royalties). Lulu also has coupons that you and your readers can use that offer discounts that do not take away from your royalty.

Pre-orders

Sadly, no. They are very behind with this and don't have any option for pre-orders at all.

Accepted Files

PDF for print and ePub or PDF for digital.

Other

- I used to prefer ordering my print books from Lulu as they have a printer in Canada. Getting author copies was a great deal when paired with one of their coupon codes that offered free shipping, but they don't seem to have a lot of free shipping codes anymore.

- Their print quality is great—I prefer their cream paper over the white. They offer both matte and glossy covers. Their hardcover books are also very nice, but are not produced in Canada so shipping costs are higher.

- You can make your print project available at all stores, just on Lulu or private just for you.

- Lulu's biggest pro is they allow revenue splitting—so if you have a co-author, you can both add your payment info and decide how to split your royalties, and they'll take care of it.

- I found Lulu weirdly strict about epub files a few years ago—files that passed the epub validator would fail at Lulu, and you got a vague message about why (e.g. "There's a problem with your NCX file"). I'd try and fix things and it wouldn't pass and their "help" people would email to state that not fixing mistakes could result in account termination. Considering I had published with them for 12 years and was begging for answers about what needed fixing, I found this tactic unsettling. I left for Draft2Digital shortly after, so I don't know if they've improved the ebook experience.

- Lots of choice for print books. There are many trim sizes, binding types and paper to choose from. Only some are eligible for distribution beyond Lulu, though, and their extended paperback royalties are very small and not worth it. Manufacturing costs for a 200–300 page book would allow you to sell for $10–15 and make a few bucks profit on Lulu—but only a few cents on Amazon (not kidding). I now recommend KDP Print for Canadians getting print on Amazon as even with only 40% royalty, it's way higher than what Lulu gets you.

- Changing cover/price/content etc is easy. Proof copies are required to be purchased only for certain changes.

- You get your own store website page to sell from and royalties are much higher here for print than through Amazon. But just try and get people to shop here ... people like their Amazon!

- Free ISBNs if you don't want to get your own. This is great for anonymity.

- I like their sales reports better than all of the other platforms.

- With Lulu, their extended print distribution outside of Lulu is all or nothing. You either distribute just to Lulu or to everywhere. You can't choose only Barnes and Noble or only Amazon etc.

- Removing your ebook from the distribution channels takes time. If you want to go into KDP Select, it can take upwards of a month or more to get off of Apple via Lulu.

- You can also make other items here – notebooks, calendars, photo books, cookbooks, yearbooks. If you have a non-standard book to publish, Lulu might work for you.

- Lulu has recently undergone a big site redesign. Things are much more modern looking and easier to find. I don't know how much the actual publishing process has changed though.

Smashwords

Acquired by Draft2Digital in 2022, this site will be integrated with D2D in the future. As of now, the site still runs separately. I'll keep this information here, but it may be worth it to use D2D from now on.

Paperback – No

Hardcover – No

Ebook – Yes

Distributes To – Apple, Nook, Kobo, Scribd, Overdrive and more. No Amazon but Smashwords offers mobi downloads on its site.

Splitting Payments - No

Tax Interview

Online tax interview

Payment Structure and Payments

Pays out monthly with no minimums, so if you make a few cents, you'll get it. Payments via PayPal are handy for Canadians.

Pricing

You can price books based on various locations in their own currency. Custom prices can be locked and changed at a later time.

Pre-orders

Yes, you can do pre-orders.

Accepted Files

Doc and ePub files.

Other

- Ebooks are sold via the Smashwords site and distributed beyond Smashwords if you choose. They do not publish to Amazon, however, they do have options to publish mobi files on their site so Kindle users could buy your book from the Smashwords site if they wanted (and knew how).

- A nice feature of Smashwords is the site allows readers to download up to 20% of the book in various file formats to see if they like it. It's a great way to try some indie authors. They also offer book files as ePub, mobi, pdf, html, txt, lrf, rtf and more. You can also gift electronic works to others via the Smashwords site.

- They have a smartphone app, so people can read on their phones.

- Smashwords provides free ISBNs or you can bring your own.

- Also gets your ebook available to libraries via Overdrive.

- You still have to get on Amazon if you want to have access to the largest marketplace, so that means managing ebooks in two locations.

- No print books, so you will have to deal with more than one publishing platform if you want print books too.

- Their publishing guidelines and requirements are a bit stricter than others, but honestly, this just helps you get your ebook in the best format possible (Apple has the most stringent guidelines, so if a site publishes to them, they'll be more stringent with the files you submit).

Other Publishing Platforms

B&N Press (Barnes and Noble)

Formerly called Nook Press, B&N Press gets your ebook and print books on the Barnes and Noble website. I have always used an aggregator to get on B&N so I have no experience with this platform. The Nook reader has never been available in Canada to my knowledge, so your Canadian audience is probably very low. Reviews have said B&N Press has better sales reports, the ability to delete old projects and a faster interface than their previous Nook Press.

Lightning Source

Owned by Ingram, they offer print-on-demand to full publishing with the same ability to be accepted into the Ingram network as IngramSpark. There are set up fees, change fees and a high cost for author copies. Like IngramSpark, you can accept returns which would allow a bookstore to order your book. Chapters/Indigo will list your books for online shoppers, but may or may not accept it on store shelves (you may have to talk to your local bookstore about that).

Streetlib

Streetlib pushes both ebook and print. They publish digitally to Google Play (one of the few aggregators that do), Amazon, Barnes and Noble, Kobo, Scribd, Tolino, Overdrive, and many more. Their print program offers the ability to print in store with Espresso machines. They offer free ISBNs and take a 10% cut.

PublishDrive

They publish to Apple, Google Play, Amazon, Apple, Kobo, Overdrive, Barnes and Noble and more. PublishDrive takes 10% of sales if you choose their royalty share option. They also have a subscription option that costs per month, but you keep all royalties. This choice is only good for those that are selling really well. PublishDrive pays you out every month, even if they haven't received money from the outlet yet.

Getting in Brick and Mortar Stores

If you are looking to get your print book into brick-and-mortar stores sites like KDP Print, Lulu, and Barnes and Noble print will not do that. Books are not listed at a 40% discount for stores through these platforms. They don't offer returns either, and for this reason no bookstore would order it. IngramSpark and Lightning Source would give stores the ability to order, but the discount and cost is not as cheap for them as it is for ordering traditionally published books, so unless you have a relationship with a particular store, and an agreement to deal with unsold stock, you will probably not be able to get into physical stores.

If you can talk with a local store, you may find one willing to help out a local author. They could order from Ingram or Lightning Source, but if you buy your own author copies (these are usually bought at cost of printing), you can sell to them for a little more and they keep the rest of the sale. You may have to agree to buy back unsold stock. You will never know unless you try, so if being in a store appeals to you, cultivate relationships with your local independent bookstore.

Do Your Research

Make sure you research any company you want to publish with. Author Solutions, the parent company of AuthorHouse, iUniverse, Tafford Publishing, Xlibris, Palibrio, and Booktango has been accused of predatory business practices and is not recommend by many advocacy groups.

Vanity presses often charge authors a lot of money up-front for publishing services that you can do yourself or hire out for at cheaper prices. Do your due diligence and research the company, the cost of services and the contracts they offer. Visit writing message boards to ask for recommendations for editors, formatting experts, marketers etc.

5

Pricing

A key thing when publishing is choosing the price of your digital book. Many POD companies and aggregators give you a lower percentage of royalties on books priced under $2.99 USD, which may be a factor in your decision-making. Deciding on price point can be affected by your genre type, word count of your book, and the going rate of self published books in general. Take some time to research so you get an idea what will work best for you.

Paperback pricing is also a bit of an art. Most books in trade paperback size retail for $9.99 to $14.99 USD, so higher prices often lead to less sales. A rule of thumb is try to match the royalty you'll receive to your ebook royalty. Paperback printing costs depend on page count, so a 200 page book at $9.99 will net you more royalties than a 300 page book at $9.99.

Many authors price the first digital book in a series lower than the rest in order to draw in readers. Some make the first book free or offer it free to their newsletter subscribers. All are valid ways to gain readers and fans, but it's up to you to decide whether you want to give away your work for the hope of gain.

One thing American authors don't think about is pricing for other nations. How many times have you picked up a book in the bookstore, looked at the $9.99 price on the back and then realized it's the U.S. price and it's $14.99 in Canada? I hate that, so I try to match my Canadian prices to the U.S. price when I can. Some outlets only allow this with digital books.

I often match the U.S. price for the U.K., Australia, New Zealand, and sometimes other European countries. The differences in exchange can make a $4.99 USD book cost between $6 to $8 in Commonwealth nations, so I like to give people a break if I can.

Promotions

Fact of self publishing life: You are going to have to promote your book.

When I first started publishing, it was fairly easy to get eyes on your book. Not many self published authors were out there, and if you priced your books below the average, people bought it. Even with amateur covers and no editing, a book had a chance.

Now there are millions of self published books on Amazon, and new ones published every day. Some authors are releasing multiple books per month to stay hot and selling. Many are using ghostwriters to pump out a ton of content. It's extremely hard to get your book noticed and hard to keep it selling once it does. Many authors have turned to marketing promotions to help readers find their books.

An unfortunate reality is that self publishing is pay to play. If you want to sell, you'll have to spend money on ads, giveaways, book tours and many other promotional tools. It's almost impossible to gain any sales or traction without paying for advertising. After 30 days, your book is no longer new, and the platforms you publish on won't be showing it as often to potential readers, so the key is selling well right out of the gate.

Here's a look at some of the most common promotions:

Mailing List Promotions

So you got your mailing list set up, but now you need subscribers.

Whatever you do, don't add your entire address book as subscribers unless you have permission from those people to be added. Mailchimp, Mailerlite and other services take permissions and spamming very seriously, and if someone reports your mailing as spam, too many of these hits can get your list and account shut down.

The easiest way to ask for subscribers is to put a link to your mailing list in the front or back matter of your book. If you check my author bio and book list page at the end of this book, you'll see a "call to action". Offering some freebies (like a free copy of your book or a free novella in your series—or even a starter library if you have multiple series) and news on new releases if you sign up are a good way to attract subscribers. You may want to put your call to action right after the book ends, or somewhere else. You might want to experiment with placement to see what works best for you.

You can also use your website to attract subscribers by putting a sign up link on the page or as a pop up. If a reader is interested enough to visit your site, they may want to connect with your newsletter.

Mailing List Builders

Services like Prolific Works, Story Origin and other list builders help authors gain subscribers to their newsletters. You upload a book and you can offer it for download, either privately or publicly. I use it privately to control who has access to my freebies for my mailing list.

The public feature allows you to join giveaways of similar genre books. With a pay account, readers that download your free book can also sign up for your newsletters. Downloads can be made contingent upon signing up or not (some giveaways require you to make it optional). At Prolific Works, a pay account is not cheap at $240 USD a year for their cheapest option. Luckily Prolific Works offers a free trial for a month where you can test out joining giveaways and getting subscribers to see how valuable it can be. During my free month my list grew from 35 people to 150 thanks to joining 3 giveaways in that month.

I struggle with mailing lists because I don't want to bother people, so I only send one out maybe once a month. I'll announce new releases or share information about my next project, but I always keep it writing related. Other authors have more personal mailing lists—it all varies across genre and between authors, so how you present yourself is really up to you. Subscribe to some in your genre and see what others are doing.

Mailing List Swaps

Some authors do swaps with authors in the same genre. If you write cozy mysteries, you and another cozy mystery author may advertise each others' books to your lists. This will often coincide with a sale on your books. It's a good way to get new sales and new readers to join your list.

Sometimes a group of authors in a genre will organize a group swap where you feature multiple authors. You may be afraid that this will pull readers away from your books and towards others, but often readers of a specific genre can be voracious. In particular, romance readers often read quickly and read everything in a certain subgenre, so you are actually opening yourself up to more readers rather than losing your own when you participate in a swap.

Amazon Advertising

Amazon Advertising is a feature where you can run ads on the Amazon website. Your book ads will utilize keywords, which you bid on. Amazon Advertising (formerly called AMS) is usually the gold standard for getting readers to see your book on the Amazon site, and are particularly useful for authors in the KDP Select program. The downside is there is a bit of a learning curve when it comes to Amazon Advertising.

Amazon Advertising ads can be complicated, but there are lots of books out there that break down how they work and how to best take advantage of them. I've linked to some in Chapter 7, but always search for the most recent books as the ad platform changes often.

Amazon Advertising has recently started tracking ad results with KDP Select, so you'll not only see if your ads have translated into sales of your books, but also page reads if your book is in KDP Select. This is a very welcome addition to their metrics.

Amazon Advertising is a great tool, but it is one that you need to stick with over time and really experiment with. You may need to try out different bid amounts, different keywords etc. It can take some time (and money) to find a combination that nets you more sales than you are spending on your ads, so be prepared that it may take some time to make back your investment in your ads.

Ebook Discovery Newsletters (BookBub etc)

Some of the most popular promotions out there are ebook discovery newsletters like BookBub, The Fussy Librarian, eReader News Today, BookRaid, Free Booksy/Bargain Booksy and many more. BookBub is the largest and most popular of these services, and also the most difficult to be accepted into—it's seen as the Holy Grail of promotions because almost everyone either makes money or at least breaks even, despite the high cost of the service (usually in the hundreds of dollars). BookBub also offers ads where you can advertize your book, but this is not the same as their feature.

These newsletters work by featuring deals for free and discounted ebooks in various genres and sending emails highlighting these deals to interested readers. Some of these companies, like BookBub, have millions—yes, *millions*—of subscribers that can see your book if you're accepted. Each service differs on how they select books— they may charge up front and everyone gets a spot, or you submit for free and only pay if you're accepted. Either way, these services get your discounted book in front of lots of readers.

Some authors will "stack" promos wherein they book a bunch of promos to run around the same time for their discounted book. This can be a great way to really boost your sales rank, but as a newbie, you may want to try the promotions one at a time, that way you have detailed information about how that promotion worked. If you do five at once and your sales spike, you won't know which was the most successful.

Facebook Ads

Facebook Ads are different from boosting posts on a Facebook page. A boosted posts makes the post you make on your page visible to more of the people who like your page and potentially people who are not fans of your page yet. I have used these in the past and find that they're only good for getting likes on your post and maybe a few likes on your page, but they don't tend to translate to clicks or buys of your book.

Facebook ads are ads you create specifically to advertise your book, and they are shown to the demographic you choose. You can narrow it down based on age, location, interests and more. If you have a book where you can compare it to something like a TV show or movie, that could be a great interest to add and could result in clicks and sell through. The key is to find a way to advertise your book that makes people want to click and buy. I've linked to a few books about ads in Chapter 7.

Blog Tours

A blog tour is a tour you can book or arrange where you provide content for other bloggers in exchange for them featuring your book. For instance, I once wrote an article about going to Las Vegas for research for my *Sin City* series for another blog. You may do cover reveals, interviews or other things for blogs, all during a short period of time (usually pre-release) to drum up attention for your books.

There are blog tour companies out there where you pay and they set up all of the blog visits. You'll be told what to provide to each and when and they take care of everything. Whether it's worth it financially is up to you. Blog tours may be more successful in some genres than others. Do some research to see if it's a good option for you.

Box Sets

A digital box set is a single file that a reader downloads that features multiple books. There are different kids of box sets: Single Author box sets often include an entire book series at a discount price from buying each book separately, while some box sets will have the first of each book in a series or a collection of standalone novels. Multi Author box sets contain material from more than one author and are often sold at a big discount to try and make a bestseller list.

Joining a multi author box set can get your books some attention, as they are quite popular and sell very well. Usually these box sets are run by one author. You often pay an entrance fee which will go toward marketing, cover, formatting etc, and then share in the royalties. Others have all the costs covered up front by the organizer, but royalties won't be paid out until the organizer has made back their investment. You'll provide a book or a novella depending on the aim of the set. It could be a theme (e.g. Christmas Sci Fi), based on length or genre. The site Bundle Rabbit is a great way to organize a box set and controls paying everyone out if you ever decide to run one yourself.

Multi author box sets can be a bit of a minefield. There have been cases of unscrupulous organizers asking those involved in box sets to engage in behaviour that would falsely inflate sales to make a best seller list. Before you join a box set, do research on the person who is running it. Make sure you get a clear contract with terms that are acceptable to you, and that the organizer knows how to deal with an author that is not American for tax purposes.

Book Trailers

A book trailer is a video that can have pictures, narration, or music and gives a reader some idea of what the vibe of your book is. Think of it like a commercial for your book. Expensive ones could be made like movie trailers with actors performing short scenes, or narration over photos. You have to ensure you're using music, pictures and other content that is free for you to use for commercial purposes.

If you have video editing talent, you can make your own book trailer, otherwise there are many companies out there that can produce one for you.

Getting Book Reviews

You may think the best way to get reviews is to ask your friends and family to read and review your book. Before you do this, be aware that it's against Amazon's Terms of Service and if they discover this (and they have their ways ...) they will delete the reviews. Amazon's algorithms can detect relationships between you and other accounts. Authors have reported that being friends with a fan via Facebook or Twitter has made a fan unable to leave reviews for their work—and that's debatable as a "relationship".

Your best bet for reviews are organic ones—ones that come from unrelated and unconnected buyers who read it and review it. These reviews may be good or bad, but one thing to remember is that reviews aren't really for you—they're for other readers. (Also ... **_never_** respond to a review, negative or positive. It's bad form for the author to stick their nose in and comment on someone's review, and nothing will mark you as an amateur so quickly).

Make sure you add a call to action in the back of your book—ask your readers to review. Both Kobo and Kindle ereaders prompt the reader to rate and review the book at the end, but even this isn't enough to get many readers to do it. When a site requires a text review, it really turns off a lot of people.

I try and direct people to Goodreads because they can leave a rating without leaving a text review. The downside to this is that Amazon reviews are really the gold standard when it comes to book reviews (and sometimes a certain number are required for you to be eligible for promotions other sites run). Amazon requires a person have ordered at least fifty dollars on the platform in the past year, so people who don't shop on Amazon much may not be able to review your book.

After organic readers, your biggest review audience is likely bloggers and reviewers that you send an ARC copy to. What's an ARC? An advanced review copy is a free copy you give to a reviewer, often before the book is released to the general public, with the understanding that they may provide a fair and unbiased review in exchange. You can't control how much they like your book or what they say about it, so you need to be comfortable with that.

You may also find reviewers via Goodreads. There are many Goodreads groups that deal with reviewing and can connect you with people willing to read and review your book for a free copy.

Before you book a promo or submit your book for one, do some Googling to see what others say about the service and decide if it's right for your book. There are many promotional companies out there, and not all will give you great results, so take the time to research ones you are interested in.

6

Self Publishing Dictionary

This is a glossary of self publishing terms that defines everything from acronyms to publishing platforms, writing terms and marketing speak.

A

Acknowledgements - The section of the front or back matter where you thank people who helped bring the book to fruition. Not a requirement.

Audible - An Amazon-owned site that offers audiobooks with a monthly subscription. Authors can submit their books via ACX.

Audiobook Creation Exchange (ACX) – A place where you can create a digital audio book. Connect with narrators to get your audiobook made. Gets you on Amazon, iTunes and Audible. You can either pay for a narrator or do a royalty share with them, where you split any royalties that come in.

Autobuy - An author whose books you buy regardless of what they are is something on your "autobuy" list - you automatically buy it.

Aggregator - A publishing aggregator publishes your book to more than one outlet. For example, Lulu.com is an aggregator that can get you on Kobo, Amazon, Nook, and more.

Also Boughts - The list of books by other authors that your readers have also bought. It can give you a good insight into what your readers like outside of your book. These are seen on the book pages on various sellers, especially Amazon.

Amazon - The biggest ebook and print book publisher on the internet, they sell print and ebooks. And everything else in the world.

Amazon Author Central - An Amazon site that allows you to claim your author profile on Amazon, write a bio, sync your blog and manage your books. You should sign up as soon as you publish a book on Amazon. Author Central is controlled at authorcentral.amazon.com. There are separate Author Central profiles/management for the UK, French, Japanese and German stores, so if you sell well in another country, you may want to sign up for their Author Central sites as well.

Amazon Advertising (formerly AMS) – This is a pay ad service used by authors to create Sponsored Ads, Sponsored Brand Campaigns and Product Display Ads for your book that show on Amazon.

Amazon Prime - A program that gives you lots of perks, like free shipping, access to TV, movies and music and the ability to borrow books for Kindle. The features vary depending on what country you're in. Customers in the U.S. and Canada get access to Prime Reading, which includes unlimited reading of Kindle Select books. Readers without Prime can sign up for Kindle Unlimited to have access to unlimited reading. Prime Reading gets you access to 1000 books available on a rotating basis, while Kindle Unlimited gets you access to over 1 million.

Advanced Reader Copy (ARC) – A free book copy given to reviewers, bloggers, etc in exchange for a fair and honest review. Some authors put together an ARC Team of readers, usually interested readers/fans from their mailing list.

ASIN – Amazon Standard Identification Number. This is a number Amazon assigns to your work to keep track of it in their system, and can be used in place of an ISBN. Google play uses their own, called a GGKEY.

Author Central – See Amazon Author Central.

Author Copy – Copies of your book you purchase at cost and can sell yourself at in-person events, conventions etc.

B

Back List – Your previously published work. Having a big back list is seen as a good sales tool. If someone likes one of your books, they'll hopefully look at the rest.

Back Matter – Material found at the back of a book, like acknowledgements, a teaser for the next book, author bio, etc.

Bar Code - The scannable code on the back of a print book, used to identify it. Most printers create the bar code for you when you have a print book made.

Barnes and Noble - A U.S.-based bookstore that sells print and ebooks. Their ebooks are for their ereader, the Nook. Also seen as BN or B&N.

Beta Reader - A person who reads a draft of your book and offers comments. Beta reading usually happens earlier in the process than editing and beta readers are usually not professional editors. You can find a friend or family member willing to beta read, as long as they're good at telling you what doesn't work.

Big Five - The five biggest U.S. traditional publishers - Hachette Book Group, HarperCollins, Macmillian Publishers, Penguin Random House and Simon and Schuster. All of them have subsidiary imprints.

BISAC Codes - Stands for Book Industry Standards and Communications. BISAC codes are universally accepted ways of categorizing your books. When you choose categories on various platforms, these categories are usually BISAC-based. Some platforms restrict you to choosing from only one top-level category (so you can choose Young Adult Fiction but not Fiction as well, so all of your subcategories will need to be under that main level heading). One day Amazon will make me happy by mirroring all of their fiction categories to BISAC codes (at least behind-the-scenes) to make our lives easier.

BKnights - A Fiverr company that offers reviews and other author services for a fee. Success varies, but it's one of the cheapest promo sites out there.

Blog tour - A virtual book tour. The author goes from blog to blog providing content, announcements, cover reveals etc. Book tours can be organized by blog tour companies for a fee.

Blurb - The summary of your book that appears on Amazon, Kobo etc. You might drive yourself crazy trying to write one.

BookBub - Provides daily emails to readers featuring discounted and free ebooks. Authors pay to feature their book, and it can be difficult to be accepted for one, but often gives a great boost in sales. BookBub is seen as the Holy Grail of marketing, as authors usually make back their investment since they have a huge database of users.

Bookfunnel - A website that allows you to upload copies of your book and to give them out in various formats to anyone you wish. It is a pay service, but is useful if you want to give out books to reviewers, as Bookfunnel handles the technical aspect. They are looking at adding a discoverability feature like Prolific Works offers.

Book Report - An online service that lets you analyze your sales information from Amazon. Free if you've made under a certain amount in royalties.

BookTok – A community of authors and readers on TikTok who discuss books. There is a big focus on YA, romance and other genre fiction. Popular videos include reviews, bookcase tours, book hauls and recommendations.

Books2Read – A free service where you can get a link for your book that shows all the stores where it's available. It's an easy way to share links to multiple stores at one time, and handy for non-American readers, as it automatically forwards them to the country-appropriate store on Amazon and Kobo.

Book trailer - A video with music, images, text and sometimes even actors that give readers a taste of what your book is about.

Bowker - A site that provides bibliographic information on published books. They issue ISBNs for Americans.

Box set - A collection that contains more than one book. The collection can be more than one book from one author (i.e., all books in a series) or books from multiple authors.

C

Calibre - A free program for managing ebooks. Calibre also features ebook creation, conversion and editing tools.

Click farm - A company that inflates buys and borrows for ebooks to improve its ranking on Amazon and other sites. It is extremely unethical to hire one, and Amazon makes an effort to remove the reviews/borrows generated from click farms and to ban users that use them. Click farms try to hide their activity by also targeting legitimate authors who can (and have) had their page reads and sales stripped after Amazon discovers it..

Cliff – Also seen as the 30 Day Cliff. Books on Amazon tend to show in more searches and rank higher in the first 30 days of their release. After 30 days, if it doesn't have sustained sales, Amazon tends not to feature it as much.

Cliffhanger – When a book ends on a moment of suspense and there are still questions about what happened. Some series authors end books with at least a small cliffhanger to keep readers interested in getting the next book. It can backfire if it takes you too long to release the next book.

Co-author – When two or more writers write a single book together. They may write separate characters (my co-author and I do this), separate chapters or have their own wonderful weird way of doing it. Co-authors are both credited for the book or they use a single pen name. My co-author and I wrote under a single pen name, then reissued the book under both of our names years later.

Cockygate – A 2018 scandal that erupted when a romance author trademarked both the word mark (an image – using a font she didn't have the rights to) and the actual word "cocky". She personally sent out cease and desist letters to authors that used the term in their book titles, pushing them to take it their book down and change the title or be sued. A lawsuit was filed, an appeal against the trademark was filed. The case was settled with the trademark being removed.

Copyediting - A copy editor checks for mistakes, inconsistencies, checks grammar, spelling and punctuation, pays attention to continuity errors, fact checking, and more.

Copypastecris - A hashtag that evolved on Twitter and refers to a Brazilian author who was found to have plagiarised from many authors, including Nora Roberts, who is suing her in Brazilian court. The case is currently ongoing.

Cover reveal - An event where an author will have an online announcement, blog post, Facebook party etc to reveal their book cover to their readers.

Cream paper - Off-white coloured paper used in printing soft and hardcover books. Amazon/KDP Print, Lightning Source and Ingram Spark cream paper is 55lbs, while Lulu cream paper is 60lbs.

Createspace - An Amazon-owned print book publishing platform that shut down in August 2018. They moved all of their print publishing to KDP Print.

Cross Promotion - When two or more authors get together to promote their work to each others' readers. Can be done with Prolific Works promotions, mailing list offerings etc. Usually done within the same genre.

D

Delivery Cost – The cost of delivering a digital file to a purchaser. Outlets will take a small percentage of the sale to cover this cost. The cost is dependent on the size of your file.

Developmental Editor – An editor whose job is to work on the structure, tone and content. Often engaged early in the process.

Draft2Digital (D2D) – A publishing aggregator that gets your ebook on Kobo, Amazon, Nook, Apple, Tolino, Overdrive and more. Often referred to as D2D.

Digital Rights Management (DRM) – This is a form of protection put on an ebook file so it can't be shared. DRM is very easy to break, so many self published authors don't both to enable DRM when you publish. Once you make the choice you can't change it.

E

Edition – A new version of an existing book. A new edition may have added information or chapters, new features or may be published by a new entity. New editions require new ISBNs.

ePub – An ebook file format that allows the ebook to be read on a compatible reader or tablet. Most non-Kindle readers use ePub files. ePubs usually contain HTML or XHTML files with the book content, CSS files for the style content, NCX for controlling how your book is displayed, an OPF file with basic information on your book. It can also contain audio, video, photo and font files. If you have web design experience with HTML, you'll probably be comfortable editing the code of an ePub.

Erotica – A book, novella etc dealing primarily with sexually arousing situations and plots that usually focus on the sexual journey of the characters. Erotica books are often hidden from the regular search on many platforms (see Erotica Dungeon).

Erotica Dungeon – aka the Dungeon. A term regarding how Amazon deals with erotic novels. They hide them from search, making them more difficult to find. Users have dubbed this the 'dungeon'. Often non erotica novels end up in the dungeon, which can negatively affect sales if the book is not an erotica novel.

Erotic Romance – Also seen as ERom, these novels focus on a romantic relationship as well as a sexual relationship, both of which are integral parts of the story.

F

Fiverr – A site where you can get almost anything (from graphics to cover design) done for five dollars (or more depending on add-ons). There are often lots of promos available via Fiverr, not all of them legit. Be very careful who you hire here—there have been cases of authors receiving plagiarized material when they hire writers from Fiverr.

Front Matter - Material that appear before the book begins, such as the copyright page, title page, dedication, introduction etc.

G

Ghostwriting - A writer that is hired to write a book that will be credited to someone else. They are usually paid for their work outright and receive no royalties. They also do not retain the rights to the book. They may have to sign a Non-Disclosure Agreement so they will not be allowed to say they wrote it.

Glossy cover - A book cover that is shiny. These are probably most common, especially in genre fiction. The alternative is a matte cover.

Goodreads - A site for readers to keep track of their books, their reading habits, and to review and rate books. Amazon owns the site. Authors can claim their author profile and use it to update and connect with readers.

Goodreads Giveaway - A pay program (that used to be free) where readers can enter to win copies of print books or ebooks. The cheapest package is $119. You are responsible for delivery of the books. (No longer worth it, in my opinion).

Google Play - Where Google/Android users get their books. Authors currently have to sign up for a wait list to get an account.

Google Play Pricing – Google Play automatically discounts your book by a certain percentage, so authors often increase the price on Google so it sells for the same amount as other platforms. See the Google Play chapter for information on how to price.

H

Happily Ever After (HEA) – The type of ending that is <u>required</u> in romance novels. Novels with romance elements without a HEA are termed love stories. Do not call your book a romance if it doesn't have a Happily Ever After at the end, because romance readers will rip you a new one for doing this.

Happy For Now (HFN) – A romance ending where the happy ending is implied but not necessarily shown or the conclusion hasn't occurred yet. You're more likely to see this in series books, where the overarching plot may not end and continue through multiple books, but there is a happy ending in some form at the end of each book.

Harem – A genre that was originally based on anime and manga that featured characters in relationships with three or more people. **Reverse harem** features a female heroine who has multiple males falling for her. Cheating isn't a part of the relationships, since the parties are all aware of each other. This genre can be seen as a sub-genre in LitRPG, romance and erotica and many other genres.

Hybrid author – An author that both self publishes and is traditionally published. They may be traditional for paperback and self publish digital for the same book, or they may have one series traditionally published and another self published. Many have an agent.

I

Indie Author - An independent author (not traditionally published) who has the rights to their own work (they haven't sold the rights to others). Many self published authors prefer using this term.

IngramSpark - A pay service to self publish your print and digital book.

Instafreebie – See Prolific Works

ISBN - The International Standard Book Number. This is the 10 or 13 digit number that identifies a specific book. An ISBN is mapped to that specific format - so a hardcover and paperback have different ISBNs. 10 digit ISBNs were used years ago, and all ISBNs issued now are 13 digits.

ITIN - The Individual Tax Payer Identification Number used to be required for non-US people to submit a W8-BEN, but you are now allowed to use the ID number from your own country (ie. a Canadian Social Insurance Number).

J

Jacket - The dust jacket cover of a hardcover book.

K

KBoards - A message board for Kindle owners that has a section for self publishers called the Writers' Cafe. I would avoid posting here if you are concerned about your writing rights—the new owners changed the Terms of Service giving themselves the right to use anything you post, like covers, text, story ideas etc. Many authors left for other communities like Writer Sanctum, Forward Motion and Facebook groups, but there is still a large contingent of posters. You may want to lurk there for info before you decide to post or not.

KDP Select - A Kindle Direct Publishing program that allows authors to list their ebook for inclusion in Kindle Unlimited and the Kindle Owners' Lending Library. You must be exclusive to Amazon (ebook only available there and nowhere else). You are paid for pages read by borrowers. Enrolment is on a 3-month at a time basis. You also get days to offer your book for free and days to offer it as a discount.

KENP - Acronym for Kindle Edition Normalized Pages. This is a page count Amazon gives your ebook so when it's in the KDP Select program, they can calculate how many pages of it were read.

Keywords – Words used to describe your book. Choosing the right keywords and keyword combos, especially on Amazon, can get you into more categories and visible in more searches. Often a trial and error process.

Kindle – An Amazon produced ereader and app for reading digital books.

Kindle Direct Publishing (KDP) – This is the platform for authors to publish ebooks and print with Amazon. It is free to use (Amazon takes a cut of any book you sell). They began a print program, KDP Print, in 2016.

Kindle Match Book – A program where someone who buys your paperback book can get a copy of your digital book for free or 99 cents. You choose this option and the amount when publishing your digital book on KDP.

Kindle Owners' Lending Library (KOLL) – Similar to KU, this program is part of Amazon Prime in the US (as Prime Reading). Prime users get access to the KOLL with their membership, allowing them to borrow 1 book per month to read. Content is the same as the KU store.

Kindle Press – Amazon's indie publishing imprint, they publish Kindle Scout novels.

Kindle Scout – An Amazon program that allowed readers to determine whether a book got published. Chosen books got their work published by Kindle Press. Amazon shut the program down in 2018.

Kindle Unlimited (KU) - For $9.99 per month, subscribers get access to Kindle Unlimited books, and can take out up to 10 at a time for free. As an author, you can get your book in this program by enrolling in KDP Select.

Kirkus Review - A site where you can request an editorial review of your book. Prices start at $425.

Kobo - An ereader and bookstore by Rakuten Kobo, its largest market is Canada.

Kobo Plus - A program you can enrol your book in if you publish via Kobo Writer's Life. It's similar to KDP Select, and pays you for page reads. The program currently only runs in two European countries.

Kobo Writer's Life - The platform to publish your ebook on Kobo.

KU - Short for Kindle Unlimited.

L

Lightning Source - A pay service to self publish your book.

Line edit - A line edit goes over the manuscript line by line, and looks for extraneous words, run-on sentences, strange phrasing, and passages that need clarification or punching up etc, as well as characterization and details.

LitRPG – Literary Role Playing Game. LitRPG is a book that is based on MMORPG – massive multiplayer online role playing games. The books feature characters in game scenarios who level up, gain gear and complete tasks. Think *Ready Player One*. These books are usually science fiction fantasy and feature a lot of RPG statistics and information.

Look Inside – A free program by Amazon that allows people to see a free sample of your book.

Loss Leader – Pricing your first book in a series lower or free to encourage people to read and buy the rest. It may sell well but net you little to no royalties.

Low Content Books – A low content book is one that, you guessed it, has low content. It may be a calendar, journal, guestbook, colouring book, crossword book etc. Something that has little writing and can be made quickly and easily.

Lulu.com – A free aggregator publishing platform that publishes print and ebooks to Amazon, Kobo, Nook, Apple, Barnes and Noble and more. They take a cut of your royalty as a fee (as do all aggregators do). They are the only platform that offers revenue splitting between co-authors.

M

Mailchimp - A mailing list website that allows you up to 2000 free mailing list members without paying. Allows you design, send and maintain an email list for free.

Mailerlite - Similar to Mailchimp, but only 1000 free members.

Mailing List - A newsletter sent out every so often by an author to announce new books, deals, events etc. Building a mailing list is seen as a common step to take when building your author brand.

Mass market paperback - A book that is pocket sized - usually around 4"x7" or so. They are not very common in self publishing.

Matte cover - A book cover that is not glossy. Matte covers often have a velvety feel, and often the blacks don't appear as dark due to the matte appearance. Some authors love this look, others don't. It's all personal taste.

Metadata - Data embedded in your ePub file that tells retailers information about your book like the title, author, genre, publisher etc.

MilSF - Military Science Fiction.

Mobi - An ebook file format. Mobi files were usually used on Kindles, but they are phasing out their use.

Mock-up - A 3D image of your book used for marketing purposes.

Multi Author Box Set - A box set that features books from more than one author. These can be in one genre, various, have a theme or not.

N

NaNoWriMo - National Novel Writing Month. A site where you can join in to write your own 50,000 words novel in the 30 days of November. Participants are Nanoers or Wrimos, depending on your preference. They also host Camp Nano in April and July.

New Adult (NA) - Books about characters in their early to mid-20s, just starting out in life. Geared to that same age group, but popular with readers of all ages, and seen most often in romance and erotica. Since many outlets don't have a New Adult category, they're often included with Young Adult (YA) books.

NCX - Navigation Control XML File. It's a file in your ePub that tells an ereader how to display your book, and is usually generated automatically by the ePub creation program.

Netgalley - A service that promotes upcoming books, usually by getting them reviews by bloggers, journalists, booksellers etc. It is not cheap to get your book on Netgalley, but you can find deals through Kobo on occasion.

Nook - The ereader sold by Barnes and Noble which is exclusive to them. Not common outside of the U.S..

O

Omnibus – A book that contains several novels, either of one series or books from multiple authors. AKA a box set.

OPF - Open Packaging Format. This is a file in your ePub that stores information about the book like the title, creator, chapter order and other identifying information.

Organic - Refers to mailing list subscribers that were not gained through a promotion - they found your list on their own because they like your stuff.

Overdrive - The ebook distribution system that some libraries use. Some ereaders (Kobo Aura One, for instance) have Overdrive integration which allows you to take out library ebooks directly from your reader if your library is part of Overdrive. Libby is their newer reading app.

Own Voices - Books that are written about a marginalized group by someone who is also a part of that group (for example, if your main character is disabled, you are also disabled). It was created as a Twitter hashtag by Corrine Duyvis to encourage diversity in authors as well as characters. You'll often see publishers on Twitter request "own voices" books.

P

Post Apocalyptic (PA) – Books that occur in a place that suffered some sort of cataclysmic event like a nuclear war or natural disaster.

Page Flip – A Kindle feature that lets a reader "pin" their current page and flip ahead to another page. There has been issue with flipped pages not being counted as read in KDP Select, but it is apparently corrected.

Page reads – Refers to how many pages a reader will read in a KU book. Payments are based on pages read. Amazon analyzes your book and assigns it a page count (KENP) based on length.

Pantser – A term that originated at the National Novel Writing Month forums, it refers to a writer that writes "by the seat of their pants" without outlines and notes. The alternatives are Plotser or Plotter.

Payment splitting – See Royalty Splitting

Permafree – Selling a book for free permanently. The thought is if you have a series, the first book being free will encourage people to read it and hopefully continue on to purchase the rest of the series.

Platform - A publishing platform is a company that provides the means necessary to put a print or ebook out for sale to the public. You can be on one platform (for instance, KDP) or multiple ones.

Plotter - A writer who relies on plot outlines, character profiles and careful planning when writing.

Plotser - A writer who uses a combo of outlines and writing by the seat of their pants. A portmanteau of plotter and pantser.

Paranormal Romance (PNR) – A romance novel with paranormal aspects.

Point five books - Books, novellas or short stories that fall between the main novels in a series - they will be numbered 1.5, 2.5 etc. Amazon doesn't include .5 books in the series pages sadly, but they are commonly found on Goodreads.

Prawn – A term referring to self published writers that don't earn a lot of money each month. The tongue-in-cheek terms were expanded by another person as follows:

- 1 figure/month: krill
- 2 figures/month: plankton
- 3 figures/month: prawn (500+ = lobster)
- 4 figures/month: trout (5000+ = rainbow trout)
- 5 figures/month: salmon
- 5 figures/month over 50k: dolphin

Pre-order - To order a book before it's on sale. You receive the book on its release day. As an author it allows you to drum up sales previous to the release. The sales usually count on the release day and not when it was pre-ordered.

Pre-made - Short for a pre-made book cover. They sell for less than a custom made cover, but there is usually no customization allowed outside of title/name.

Price match - When a platform (usually Amazon) matches the price of your book to a (usually) lower price found on another platform. Commonly sought by authors when they price their book free at some platforms in hopes Amazon will price match it to free there as well - Amazon doesn't allow you to set your book to free on your own unless you're in the KDP Select program.

Print on Demand (POD) - A company that prints a copy of a book when it's purchased, instead of printing tons of copies and hoping they sell. It has allowed people to write and publish their own books without having any overhead like buying tons of copies and trying to sell them yourself. Companies like Lulu, Smashwords, Draft2Digital, Kindle Direct Publishing and more are print on demand publishers.

Prolific Works - Formerly known as Instafreebie. A site that allows you to offer a free sample or book to readers. The books are searchable and discoverable on the site if you want them to be. Readers sign up and can request copies of the books you post. There are often theme packages to attract readers. For instance, they might have a group offerYoung Adult Fantasy books and you can sign up to include your book in that promo.

Promos - Short for promotion. Buying featured status for your book somewhere. Most promos send out a list of discounted or free books to their mailing list subscribers. BookBub has millions of subscribers, so finding a good promotional site that will accept your book is a good way to get more readers.

Promoted Post - A paid Facebook option to boost the visibility of a post. It often doesn't result in much more attention gained.

Pronoun - A self publishing service that shut down in 2017.

Proof Copy - A copy an author goes over to check for errors. Amazon proof copies are stamped on the cover with the word "PROOF" so they can't be sold. I usually buy the author copy versions so if I want to give it away to someone after I can.

Proofreading - A proofreader checks the printed book against the official edited manuscript to make sure everything is correct.

Q

None yet.

R

Rafflecopter – A site that helps you run an online giveaway by automating a lot of the process.

Rank – How your book ranks against others in sales and page reads. The lower the number, the better the rank.

Reader magnet – An offering to attract a reader to your books – usually a free book, like a prequel or book 1 in a series, or a starter library. Can be similar to a loss leader if it's priced lower than other books.

Revenue splitting – See Royalty Splitting

Reverse harem – See Harem.

Romancelandia – The romance genre fandom, especially those in the online world of blogs and Twitter. Romance readers are voracious and have been the ones catching many of the plagiarism issues in the romance genre.

Royalties – The money you make from the sale of your book. Most publishing programs take a small cut of each ebook or print book sale to cover their costs, and you receive the rest. This is your royalty.

Royalty Splitting – Where royalties are split between two or more people (usually co-authors). Each author will get a percentage of the royalty. Not many platforms offer this at the moment. Also called Revenue Splitting or Payment Splitting.

S

Scribd - A monthly subscription service for ebook and audiobooks.

Scrivener - A pay writing program that allows for lots of planning and plotting and exports to ePub. Very popular with many authors for the ease of story planning, writing and ebook creation.

Series - A collection of books featuring the same characters. They may take place one after another (like the *Harry Potter* series) or be, in essence, standalone books with the same characters (like the *Nancy Drew* series). Series are seen as easier to market than standalone books.

SF - Stands for Science Fiction, which deals with science and imaginative concepts that usually involve space, extraterrestrials, the future and/or technology. Also seen as Sci Fi.

Sigil - A free program that allows you to create and edit ePub files.

Single Author Box Set - A box set that features books from just one author. The books may be an entire series, or first books in a series, or all of an author's books.

Smashwords - An ebook-only self publishing platform that has extended distribution just about everywhere but Amazon. They are merging with Draft2Digital in the near future.

Stacked promos – When you book a bunch of promotions to run concurrently or one after the other. Many authors do this when they get a BookBub feature.

Standalone – A novel that is not part of a series.

Starter library – Some authors offer a collection of their ebooks to people who subscribe to their newsletters. They usually include the first books in their series or related short stories or novellas.

Steamy – Term for romances with more sex, but don't fall into erotica territory. It may run close to erotic romance.

Sticky – To have a book selling well and at a good chart position for an extended period of time. It is "stuck" on the charts. This is a good thing, you want your book to be sticky.

Street team – A team of people put together by an author, usually from mailing list members, who will be ARC readers, and sometimes assist with getting the word out about a new release on social media etc.

Stripping – Short for "page read stripping" it's when KDP adjusts the income of writers in the KDP Select program after going through the read data and removing any suspicious reads. So you may think you've made $100 this month in reads, but then $32 of them are stripped away because Amazon determined they weren't legitimate.

Subgenre - Sub categories of your book genre. For instance, your book may be a romance, but it's subgenre may be sweet romance or alpha male romance. It narrows down the type of you book write and helps readers find what they're looking for.

Sweet/clean - Terms used for romance books that are not racy and don't contain sex. The preferred term is sweet, since "clean" indicates that books with sex are somehow "dirty".

T

Tail - The length of time your sales stay high or good after a promo. A long tail is good, it means people are continuing to buy your book or your other books long after the promo is over.

Table Of Contents (TOC) - All ebooks must have a Table of Contents so readers can navigate within the book with their ereader. Many books have them at the beginning and the end.

Trade paperback - A book that is larger than a mass market (pocket) size. They vary between 5"x8" and 6"x9". Traditionally they were soft cover versions of the hardcover book, and the same size as the hardcover (which are usually 6"x9").

Traditionally Published - An author published by a publishing house or indie press. Traditionally published authors usually have agents.

Trim Size - The size of a print book. Common trim sizes are trade paperback (from 5"x8" to 6"x9") and mass market paperback (4 1/4" x 7").

U

Urban - Largely written for and by African Americans, the genre usually focuses on city life and socio-economic issues.

UF - Urban Fantasy. Set in the city, but focusing on fantasy elements/characters etc.

V

Vanity Press - A company that will charge an author money to publish their book. Don't go with a vanity press.

Vellum - A Mac-based program which allows you to create ebooks.

Verified Purchase - A designation used on Amazon to show that a reviewer actually bought the book in question. KU borrows don't show as verified purchases.

W

W-8BEN - A tax form for Canadian authors to fill out and send to the platform that informs the publishing platform how much in royalties to withhold for U.S. taxes – none!

Wide - A term used by authors to indicate they aren't exclusive to Amazon and sell their ebooks elsewhere as well. Also seen as "going wide" when an author says they may take their books out of KDP Select to sell on other platforms.

Withholding - Money that a publishing program withholds from the author to pay US taxes. If you are non-U.S., and your country has a tax treaty with the US that covers royalties, your withholding may be less than the 30% the US takes. In order to stop the withholding, there are U.S. tax forms to send in or an online tax interview to fill out. See W-8BEN.

Wordpress - A blogging/website platform. Two versions exist, the free .com site and the self-hosted .org. The .com has pay packages to allow use of a domain name as well.

Wraparound - A print book cover that is one file - a front, spine, and back cover.

Write to market - When an author researches popular genres and what's selling, and then writes a book in a related subgenre that is currently underserved, in hopes their book will become a bestseller. Other authors may write what they like and worry about how to market it after (um, hi).

Writer Sanctum - A message forum for self publishing authors to ask questions, get feedback etc. Some of the forums are private for members, others are public.

X

X-Ray - X-Ray for Authors is a Kindle feature that allows readers to learn more about a subject while reading by tapping and holding on a word or phrase. As an author, you can add your own definitions, descriptions and information for your readers. You can turn the feature off and on for each book.

Y

Young Adult (YA) - Books aimed at teenage readers, but enjoyed by all age groups. They usually feature teenage characters dealing with things that would affect that age group. YA can be "lower" (aimed at the 13-15 age group) or "higher" (aimed at the 16 and over group).

Z

None yet.

7

In Closing

This book is just a short introduction to the self publishing world. As Canadians, we're lucky that we can easily appeal to the mass audience in the United States as well as Canada without too much difficulty. The trade off is having to deal with a few extra things Americans don't ... but we are lucky to be able to get free ISBNs, not be taxed withholding like other countries, and have an overall easier time of it than some other nations.

Publishing can be stressful, but hopefully this book will have helped you sort out some of the Canadian-specific issues you probably won't read about anywhere else. Here is a list of other books and helpful sites that can assist you on your self publishing journey.

BOOK RECOMMENDATIONS

All of the authors listed here are self published and their books are born from their experience in the trenches. All of these ebooks are available on Kobo and Amazon (as well as other retailers) unless noted.

Writing

5000 Words Per Hour: Write Faster, Write Smarter (Chris Fox)
The fastest way to succeed as an author is to write more books. How do you do that with a day job, family, school or all your other time commitments? The secret is efficiency. 5K WPH will help you maximize your writing time by building effective habits that both measure and increase your writing speed.

Let's Get Digital (David Gaughran)
Learn how to self publish your book and build an audience through social media, ads, and other marketing strategies.

Lifelong Writing Habit: The Secret To Writing Every Day (Chris Fox)
Lifelong Writing Habit draws on well tested neuroscience to help you install a daily writing habit that will endure for life.

Plot Gardening: A Simple Guide to Outlining Your Novel (Chris Fox)

Whether you are a first time novelist, or a seasoned author, Plot Gardening will teach you the fundamentals of storytelling, delivered in a practical way.

Write To Market: Deliver A Book That Sells (Chris Fox)
This book will teach you to analyze your favourite genre to discover what readers are buying, to mine reviews for reader expectations, and to nail the tropes your readers subconsciously crave.

Writing The Other (Nisi Shawl, Cynthia Ward)
If you are writing a character unlike yourself (a different race, ability level, health situation), this book can help you navigate those waters.

The Writers Helping Writers Series (Becca Puglisi and Angela Ackerman)
A collection of 9 guide books: The Emotion Thesaurus, The Negative Trait Thesaurus, The Positive Trait Thesaurus, The Rural Setting Thesaurus, The Urban Setting Thesaurus, The Emotional Wound Thesaurus, The Occupation Thesaurus, and the two volume The Conflict Thesaurus.

Save The Cat Writes A Novel (Jessica Brody)
Offers tips on making your writing more compelling and illustrates major story beats.

General Publishing Guides

Let's Get Digital: How To Self Publish and Why You Should (David Gaughran)

Publish like a pro and start finding readers today with the most comprehensive and up-to-date self-publishing guide on the market.

Book Launches

Launch To Market: Easy Marketing For Authors (Chris Fox)

Launch to Market provides a simple system to plan, track, and execute your book launch. It covers the basics of marketing in an easy to understand way, complete with exercises that will prepare you for your best launch ever.

Relaunch Your Novel: Breathe Life Into Your Backlist (Chris Fox)

Have you launched a novel, or many novels, only to have them land with a whimper? Have you had a great selling book or series slowly fade away to obscurity? What if you could relaunch those books, turning your backlist into a great source of income?

Marketing

AMS Ads For The Rest Of Us (A. Sharpe)

AMS Ads for the Rest of Us provides an easy to understand, light-hearted approach, empowering you to create ads that will draw your ideal readers to your books. This book is available on Amazon only.

Newsletter Ninja: How to Become an Author Mailing List Expert (Tammi Labrecque)
Newsletter Ninja is a comprehensive resource designed to teach you how to build and maintain a strongly engaged email list—one full of actual fans willing to pay for the books you write, rather than free-seekers who will forget your name and never open your emails.

Six Figure Author: Using Data to Sell Books (Chris Fox)
Amazon has spent billions of dollars over the last decade building the world's best sales engine. They use machine learning to sell massive piles of books, and that engine is just waiting for you to tap into it. This is the book that will teach you how.

Bookbub Ads Expert (David Gaughran)
Learn all about Bookbub's ad system and how to craft the perfect ad to sell your book.

Strangers to Superfans: A Marketing Guide to the Reader Journey (David Gaughran)
Strangers to Superfans puts you in the shoes of your Ideal Readers, and forces you to view your marketing from their perspective.

About The Author

Jennifer Samson (she/her) is the author of the coming-of-age *Sin City* series and co-author of the dark comedy/thriller *The Final Cut*, the first in the *Billie and Diana* series. She has also authored the best selling *Self Publishing for Canadians*, a non fiction guide to self publishing with a Canadian flair. She has been published in the literary journals *Thursday* and *The Lyre*, as well as the BoldPrint book *Friends*. Her work has been featured in the Brookline TAB, Toronto Star, Ottawa Citizen and Edmonton Sun.

She enjoys fine-nibbed pens, Hilroy loose leaf paper, corner store candy, adorable cats, and beating her Goodreads Reading Challenge every year. Being Canadian, a love of hockey goes without saying. Although sometimes the Canucks make that love very, very difficult.

She is a member of Gamma Xi Phi, a predominantly African American, anti-racist, non-hazing, all-gender professional fraternity for artists and creators.

She currently resides on the unceded territory of the Sḵwx̱wú7mesh (Squamish), Səl̓ílwətaʔ/Selilwitulh (Tsleil-Waututh) and xʷməθkʷəy̓əm (Musqueam) Coast Salish peoples.

* * *

Books by Jennifer Samson

SIN CITY SERIES
Crime/Love Story

Piece of Work
Sin City
Tilt*
The Dead Woman
Neon and Tinsel*
Bayou Bound

*with MB Miller

Coming Soon:

Under The Gun

BILLIE AND DIANA SERIES

with M.B. Miller
Comedy/Thriller

The Final Cut

Coming Soon:

Curtains

www.ingramcontent.com/pod-product-compliance
Lightning Source LLC
LaVergne TN
LVHW051131080426
835510LV00018B/2351